Practical
MIDI handbook

Second edition

R A Penfold

PC Publishing

PC Publishing
4 Brook Street
Tonbridge
Kent

Second edition 1990
Reprinted 1992

© PC Publishing

ISBN 1 870775 13 9

British Library Cataloguing in Publication Data

Penfold, R.A.
  Practical MIDI handbook – 2nd ed
  1. Music. Applications of microcomputer systems
  I. Title
  780.285416

  ISBN 1–870775–13–9

Phototypeset by Scribe Design, Gillingham, Kent
Printed in Great Britain by BPCC Wheatons Ltd, Exeter

Preface

The musical instrument digital interface (MIDI) is a subject that is surrounded by a great deal of misunderstanding, and total myth for that matter. Apparently, some people have bought computers which have a MIDI interface under the impression that in order to obtain music from it they only need to connect the MIDI "OUT" socket to a hi-fi system! Much of the manufacturers literature that accompanies MIDI equipment is more reminiscent of scientific papers than users' manuals. Although MIDI is admittedly a fairly technical subject, gaining an understanding of it is not such a daunting task as one might imagine. Provided things are explained clearly and in logical order that is, which is the purpose of this book.

Like the very successful first edition of the Practical MIDI Handbook, this second edition is primarily aimed at musicians who wish to exploit the vast capabilities of MIDI, but have no previous knowledge of electronics or computing. The basics of MIDI are explained, including such things as interconnecting a system, and just why MIDI is needed at all. However, the majority of the book is devoted to an explaination of just what MIDI can do, and how to exploit it to the full. This includes the fundamentals of control codes, details of the types of equipment and software that are currently available, and how systems can be tailored to suit individual requirements.

The main emphasis is on actually connecting up and using MIDI systems rather than the theory, but the subject is covered in depth, and technical details are there for those who need them. For example, full details of the MIDI code numbers are provided for the benefit of those who wish to undertake their own MIDI programming. Advice on deciphering the technical information in equipment manuals is also provided!

MIDI is a fairly rigid standard, and as such it does not change much from one year to the next. However, this second edition has been expanded to include details of developments such as the all-important 'multi' mode, MIDI standard files, developments in computers and MIDI software, the increased sophistication of modern MIDI instruments, and a few additions to the MIDI specification.

Contents

1 Why MIDI?

Those who are not familiar with the detailed workings and capabilities of the musical instrument digital interface (MIDI) often question whether it is really a development of much significance. After all, it is just a means of swapping information between suitably equipped electronic musical instruments, and it does not provide new sounds that were previously impossible. Also, it was possible to couple together two or more instruments before MIDI came into existence. MIDI is often used for computer control of instruments, but even this was possible in the pre-MIDI era.

If we first consider things on a very superficial level, the main advantage of MIDI is that it is a true standard. It has been adopted by a large number of manufacturers, and any instrument or controller that has a set of MIDI sockets will work perfectly well with any other piece of MIDI equipment from any manufacturer. Not all instruments are MIDI equipped, but it is now a requirement for any synthesizer or sound sampler if it is to be considered as anything other than a 'toy' instrument by the electronic music fraternity. In fact MIDI sockets are now to be found on a wide range of gear, including drum machines, electronic pianos, effects units, mixers, and even a few portable keyboards. This gives a degree of versatility that was never provided by earlier methods of interfacing. Although some combinations of equipment will not fully exploit the features of every instrument in the setup, the MIDI standard ensures that there is at least a good basic level of operation. In most cases the MIDI system is sufficiently standardized to permit sophisticated operation of every element in the system.

With today's instruments becoming ever more complex, another advantage of MIDI that should not be overlooked is that it provides a simple means of obtaining complex interconnection between instruments. Older methods of interfacing generally required large numbers of connecting cables in order to achieve what was often a relatively crude degree of control.

Pre-MIDI

I will not dwell at great length on methods of interfacing prior to the arrival of MIDI, but it is helpful to have at least a basic understanding of these earlier methods. They show the types of communications that a musical instrument interface must provide. MIDI can seem to be a very long solution to a short problem, but the inadequacies of earlier methods put the usefulness and versatility of MIDI into perspective.

In the pre-MIDI era it was quite common for two synthesizers to be connected together so that both instruments could be played from the keyboard of one of them. The more simple analogue synthesizers tended to have a rather 'thin' sound, and using two instruments together permitted much 'thicker' or 'fatter' sounds to be obtained. Either way, the sound was much richer, and stood better comparison to acoustic instruments. With the more complex synthesizers there was perhaps a less dramatic improvement to be gained, but two instruments in unison could still produce a better range of sounds than each individual instrument used in isolation.

Many analogue synthesizers are monophonic (i.e. can only play one note at a time), and when two of these are connected together they still provide only monophonic operation. They will both play the same note, or in most cases it would be possible to tune the slave instrument to play up to at least one octave higher or lower than the master instrument. Proper polyphonic operation with two completely independent notes at a time requires the two-handed approach to playing.

The normal method of interconnecting two analogue synthesizers is the gate/CV method. This requires two jack leads to interconnect the two instruments, giving an arrangement of the type outlined in Fig. 1.1. Fig. 1.2 gives a more detailed version of this setup. In some cases the switches are contacts on the sockets, that are operated automatically when a plug is inserted into or removed from the socket. The gate signal is derived from keyboard switches, and with most instruments this signal is normally at about zero volts, and goes to around +4 to 5 V when a key is pressed.

Lost touch
Most analogue synthesizers have an ADSR (attack, decay, sustain, release) envelope shaper, and pressing a key controls the volume of the note as shown in Fig. 1.3. First the volume builds up to maximum

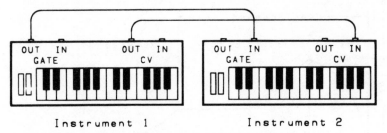

Figure 1.1 The basic interconnections for analogue synthesizers

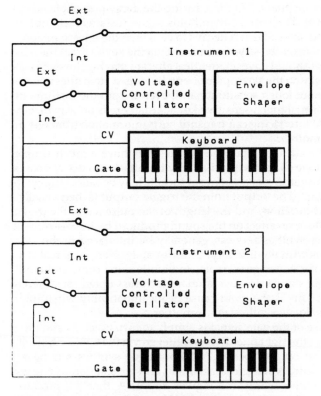

Figure 1.2 Internal/external switching arrangement of the gate/CV system (the switching is sometimes automatic)

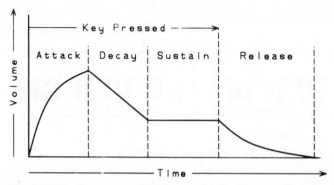

Figure 1.3 The four part envelope used on most analogue synthesizers

during the attack phase, but then during the decay phase it falls back to a lower level. The volume then holds at the sustain level until the key is released, after which it decays to zero over the release period.

Playing a note on the slave instrument via the keyboard of the master instrument should have an identical effect to playing the same note in the same way on the slave instrument. But this system does not provide any form of touch sensitivity and, even if both the instruments have some form of touch sensitive keyboard, there is no way that the basic gate/CV interfacing can transmit such information from one instrument to another.

Some of the cheaper analogue synthesizers have a much simpler form of envelope shaper which has only the attack and decay phases. With these the gate input and output sockets may be called 'trigger in' and 'trigger out'. The output from the trigger output is then usually a pulse of fixed duration, and the length of the pulse fed to the trigger input has little or no effect on the sound produced by the instrument. These simpler synthesizers can generally be interfaced to the more complex types with no difficulty. Unfortunately, there is no real standardization of gate/trigger signals, and while some conform to ordinary 5 V logic standards, several manufacturers opted for different signal levels. This is the main cause of incompatibility when interfacing one analogue synthesizer to another.

The purpose of the gate signal is simply to turn notes on and off; it does not select the right one. This is achieved via the CV (control voltage) input and output sockets. Most analogue synthesizers have a logarithmic control voltage characteristic, and the standard is one volt per octave. In other words, if 3 V gives middle A, then 4 V produces the A one octave above middle A, and 5 V would give the A one octave above this. In terms of semitones, the control voltage must be raised by about 83.33 mV (0.08333 V) per semitone. Fig. 1.4 shows the keyboard to voltage relationship for this system. Logarithmic scaling gives quite accurate pitch control and enables a wide range of notes to be accommodated (as much as 10 octaves in some cases).

Unfortunately, there is also a lack of standardization of CV signals. Most instruments, especially the more recent ones, conform to the 1 volt per octave logarithmic standard. However, some instruments have a linear control characteristic. In other words, if 3 V gives middle C, then 6 V would produce the C one octave above middle C, and 12 V would give the C one octave above this. This system is more easily implemented, since voltage controlled oscillators (VCOs) usually have a linear control characteristic. Logarithmic control is obtained by adding a converter circuit ahead of the oscillator. The point of doing this is that with linear control and wide compass, either very small voltages are going to be involved at the lowest octaves, or the voltage to give the highest note will be quite high. Neither of these options is attractive as far as interfacing instruments is concerned. Very low voltages leave the system vulnerable to stray pick-up of mains hum or other electrical noise, and high voltages are undesirable from the safety aspect. The linear and logarithmic synthesizers are totally incompatible, although it is quite possible to convert one characteristic to the other with the aid of some not terribly complex electronics.

Limitations

One obvious problem of the gate/CV system is that it lacks sophistication. Some manufacturers tried to give greater versatility by including

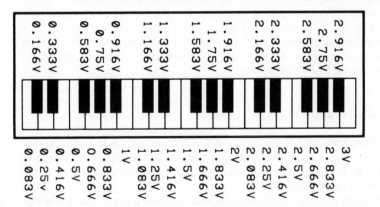

Figure 1.4 The 1 volt per octave system adopted by many analogue synth manufacturers

more inputs and outputs, such as CV inputs and outputs for the filters. Even if the industry had settled on true standards for the CV and gate signals, and had all provided additional inputs and outputs, it is difficult to imagine this system surviving long enough to be adopted in modern instruments.

What is ultimately the fatal flaw in the gate/CV system is the large number of connecting wires that are required. Compatibility problems apart, it is easy enough to connect one monophonic synthesizer to another, and with a suitable interface it is even possible to achieve computer control of one synthesizer without too much difficulty. The problems really mount when this system is applied to polyphonic operation. It is not uncommon for modern instruments to have eight or even 16 note polyphony. Even with just the basic gate and CV signals and no extras, this would need 16 or 32 leads to control each instrument! With further connections for the control of filters etc. the situation would be even worse. A computer or some other micro-controller is at the heart of many current electronic music systems, and providing a large number of control outputs for one of these, while not very difficult technically, would be relatively costly. A system having a mass of cables might be quite good for impressing your friends, but it is not very practical. It is something that is certainly far from ideal for use on the road!

As more and more polyphonic instruments were produced at increasingly attractive prices, it became apparent to instrument designers that an improved method of interfacing was needed. What was required was a system that would avoid the need for masses of cables, but which would permit sophisticated multi-channel operation. The system also needed to be sufficiently versatile to accommodate a wide range of different types of instruments, effects units, controllers, and other types of equipment. This includes drum machines, with their synchronization requirements. It also needed to have a reasonable chance of accommodating new developments that would inevitably come along from time to time.

Synchronization

Synthesizers are not the only pre-MIDI instruments to have interfacing facilities. Drum machines also have sockets to permit two or more units to be used together, but the method of interfacing is totally different to the gate/CV type.

A drum machine produces a repetitive drum pattern, and the tempo is controlled by an internal clock circuit. This is merely a circuit that provides electrical pulses at regular intervals. For this system to work properly, the length of time from the start of one pulse to the start of the next must be quite short so that the rhythm can be produced accurately. Drum beats are commenced only at the beginning of clock pulses. Fig. 1.5 shows a typical relationship between the clock signal and the output signals (which are on three channels in this case).

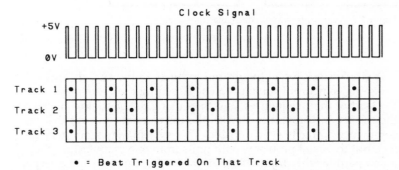

Figure 1.5 The triggering of a drum machine's voices is strictly synchronized to a clock pulse signal

Using a single drum machine is quite straightforward, since it is just a matter of setting the desired tempo and then playing along in time with the drum rhythm. Things are more difficult if two drum machines are to be used simultaneously. The obvious way of doing things is to set one instrument to the required tempo, and then to carefully adjust the second drum machine to synchronize it with the first one. This sounds simple, but in practice it would be very difficult to get them properly synchronized in the first place, and they would almost certainly creep out of synchronization before too long even if they could be set up correctly initially. Adding a third drum machine to the system would make such a setup even more impracticable.

The problem is solved by providing drum machines with clock or synchronization inputs and outputs. A system with two drum machines would be connected as shown in Fig. 1.6. A number of slave units can be connected into the system if desired. It is just a matter of switching each one for operation with an external clock, and feeding its clock input from the clock output of the master instrument. This requires a 'split' cable that wires together several plugs, or a junction box which splits the single output of the drum machine into several outputs so that each one can drive a separate clock input (as in Fig. 1.7).

7

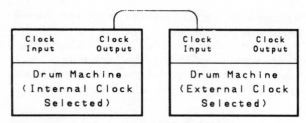

Figure 1.6 A conventional twin drum machine setup

A single clock for all the drum machines in the system solves the 'creeping' synchronization problem. Resetting the drum machines to the start of their sequences, and then using the start/stop switch on the master instrument to start all the instruments ensures that they commence correctly synchronized. This system may seem to be perfect, but there are problems with units from one manufacturer being incompatible with drum machines from other manufacturers. In particular, some machines operate with 24 clock pulses per beat, whereas others use 48, 96, or whatever. A limitation of this system is that it can only be stopped and started manually. It works well if the drum pattern is required throughout a piece, but it is rather cumbersome if the drum accompaniment must be repeatedly switched in and out.

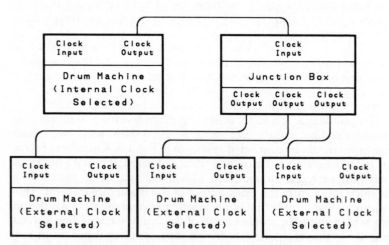

Figure 1.7 The setup used to synchronize several drum machines

Serial interface

MIDI was not the only system put forward as a successor to earlier methods, but it is the only one that has gained wide acceptance. All the main electronic musical instrument manufacturers now support the MIDI system. It first emerged in 1982, and it was the result of discussions the previous year involving a number of electronic instrument manufacturers, including Roland, SCI, Yamaha and Korg. A lack of standardization in the hi-fi and video fields had resulted in some loss of public confidence in electronic goods in general, and the electronic music scene had not been without incompatibility problems in the past. MIDI was the manufacturers' response to a clear need for a properly standardized interface for the new generations of more sophisticated instruments. MIDI has evolved over the intervening years, but it remains essentially the same as it was in 1982. MIDI was designed to avoid the rapid obsolescence that has overtaken so many recent pieces of electronics, and so far it seems to have been successful in this respect.

There are two sides to MIDI – the hardware and the software. The hardware is the electronics that passes information from one instrument to another, and the software is the system of coding used to place what are often quite complex instructions into what are really quite simple electrical signals. The problem with the old gate/CV system was that it required a large number of connecting cables, and lacked versatility. MIDI overcomes both of these drawbacks.

Starting with the lack of cables, the gate/CV system is a form of parallel communications system. All this means is that a separate connecting wire is used for each set of data that is transmitted. The obvious way of reducing the number of connecting leads is to use some form of serial interface, where all the signals are sent along a single cable. Obviously they can not all be sent at once, and information for each channel has to be transmitted in turn. In fact information for each channel has to be sent a bit at a time, as gate and note value information can not be sent simultaneously. There are problems when using this serial approach with electronic instruments, particularly with large systems where vast amounts of information must be exchanged. A fairly high operating speed is needed to avoid a lack of synchronization between channels, or a situation where the system simply can not cope with the amount of information that must be exchanged. However, the drawbacks are relatively minor when compared to the advantages. Few of us are likely to own such a complex array of equipment that the MIDI system will be unable to cope!

To use MIDI equipment successfully you do not really need a

9

detailed knowledge of the way in which the information is sent down the cables. It is helpful to know that MIDI transmits data in the form of numbers, which are always integers (whole numbers) from 0 to 255. This may seem to offer very limited scope, but where complex information must be exchanged more than one number can be used. For example, the first number could indicate that a note on a certain channel should be turned on, the next number could indicate which note, and the next could indicate the loudness of the note. This idea of information being exchanged in the form of code numbers or groups of numbers is central to an understanding of MIDI.

A full explanation of the MIDI version of serial interfacing is provided for those who are interested in the technicalities. Those who are not may prefer to skip over this section and go straight onto the one dealing with MIDI interconnections.

It would be possible to have a serial system that was an exact equivalent to the gate/CV method. This would work by having a pulse to indicate the beginning of a note, followed by the control voltage, and then another pulse to indicate the end of the note. A system such as this is rather clumsy though, and it lacks versatility. It could not easily be made to handle more than one channel for example.

Musical digits

MIDI is a purely digital system, and it does not rely on a varying voltage to indicate a note value, or anything else. The signal voltage is either logic 0 or logic 1. The gate signal of an analogue synthesizer is actually an example of a simple digital signal. For an instrument that uses ordinary 5 V logic levels, the gate signal is normally at logic 0 ('low', or at about 0 to 1 V), and it switches to logic 1 ('high' or about +4 to +5 V) when a key is pressed. One digital signal on its own is of little use in most applications, since it only provides a simple on/off indication. Several digital signals grouped together give much greater versatility, and they are normally used in groups of eight (or multiples of eight). Each individual signal in the group is called a 'bit' (an abbreviation of 'binary digit'), and a group of eight bits is called a 'byte'.

Bit by bit

For those readers who are not familiar with the binary system of numbering, an explanation of how 0s and 1s can be used to represent a decimal number such as 156 will help. With the decimal numbering system the digits indicate the number of units, tens, hundreds, etc. A similar approach is used with the binary numbering system, but the digits indicate the number of units, twos, fours, eights, sixteens, etc. This is the best that can be managed when each digit can only be a 1 or a 0.

Any number can be handled by the binary numbering system, but it takes a lot of digits to represent numbers of quite modest magnitude. For instance, the decimal number of 156 mentioned above would be 10011100 in binary. The chart explains this in greater detail.

128s		64s		32s		16s		8s		4s		2s		1s		
1		0		0		1		1		1		0		0		
128	+	0	+	0	+	16	+	8	+	4	+	0	+	0	=	156

An eight bit byte can only handle numbers from 0 to 255 (11111111 in binary), but this is adequate for most purposes. However, as pointed out previously, it is sometimes necessary to use a group of bytes in order to send complex information.

Using logic circuits to represent binary numbers is obviously no problem, with each output representing one digit of the number. Incidentally, the bit which represents the units is often referred to as the LSB (least significant bit) while the bit which represents the highest value (the 128s bit in this case) is commonly called the MSB (most significant bit).

Using one output as a source of multi-bit binary numbers may seem to be impossible, but it can be done. In fact it is a standard process these days. It is just a matter of placing the data onto the output literally bit by bit, with the receiving device reading the bits one by one and reassembling them into a complete byte. The problem with this method is synchronizing the transmitting and receiving equipment, as it is clearly essential that the receiving device always knows which bit of which byte it is reading. One approach is the 'synchronous' type, where there is a second signal line that provides some form of timing signal to the receiving equipment.

This is not the method used in the MIDI system though. Instead an asynchronous link is used, and this has the timing signals and the data both sent on the same line. Fig. 1.8 helps to explain how this system operates. Under standby conditions the output is at logic 0, but when a byte is commenced it goes to logic 1 for a certain period of time. This is called the 'start bit', and it is a timing signal. It indicates to the receiving equipment that the state of the connecting line must be tested at regular intervals thereafter. The start bit is followed by the data which is placed onto the output one bit at a time, starting with the least significant bit, and working through in sequence to the most significant bit. Finally, there is a stop bit. This is a further timing bit,

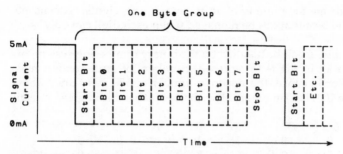

Figure 1.8 The standard byte used in the MIDI specification has one start bit, eight data bits (numbered zero to 7) and one stop bit. Most MIDI instructions consist of between one and three of these bytes, and they are transmitted round the system at a rate of 3000 bytes per second

and it merely ensures that there is a reasonable gap between one byte of data and the next.

Serial systems of this type are much used in computing and electronic communications systems. In fact the standard RS232C serial interface is very similar to MIDI technically. With RS232C systems there is always one start bit, but there can be anything from five to eight data bits, and one, one and a half, or two stop bits. Additionally, there can be a parity bit which operates as a part of a simple error checking system. Fortunately, MIDI is much more standardized, and the only word format used is one start bit, eight data bits, one stop bit, and no parity. Although there is no checking that data has been correctly received, you will soon know if there has been an error as the sounds from the instrument concerned would almost certainly make it all too obvious. Errors are very rare in practice though, and the added complexity of a system of error detection and correction is not really justified.

Crystal clear

Of course, the reliability of a system of this type depends on the rate at which the transmitting apparatus outputs bits being accurately matched by the rate at which the receiving equipment reads them. In practice, the timing at each end of the system is normally controlled by a quartz oscillator (as used in many clocks and watches). These ensure a high degree of accuracy. In fact they generally provide far greater accuracy than the minimum requirement for reliable operation. With a synchronization signal being sent at the beginning of each byte an error of a few percent should not cause the transmitter and receiver to creep out of synchronization by the final bit of each byte. Crystal oscillators are generally accurate to within about 0.001%!

Originally MIDI used a speed of 19200 bits per second or 'baud' to use the correct term. You may also encounter the term 'kilobaud', which is one thousand baud. 19200 baud is therefore the same as 19.2 kilobaud. This may seem a rather odd figure to choose, but it is the highest standard rate for RS232C serial systems. Before MIDI was launched commercially the baud rate was increased to 31250 baud (31.25 kilobaud) as the original data transfer rate was deemed too slow. This might again seem like an odd figure to settle on, but it is what you get if you divide one million by 32. This makes it a convenient figure for the hardware designer who can use standard frequency crystals in the hardware.

A speed of 19200 baud might actually seem to be perfectly all right, but a point to bear in mind is that this is 19200 *bits* per second, not 19200 *bytes* per second. With ten bits (including start and stop types) being required per byte, it therefore only corresponds to a maximum of about 1920 bytes per second. It also has to be remembered that some MIDI instructions take several bytes. Even the higher rate finally selected only gives a little over 3000 bytes per second at best. This is more than adequate for most MIDI systems, but it could give a slight loss of synchronization on a multi-channel system when there is a great deal of activity taking place.

In isolation

MIDI is different from the RS232C system in the way that signals are coupled from one piece of equipment to another, and it is not usually possible to interface a MIDI port directly to an RS232C port. The RS232C system uses voltages of about plus and minus 12 V to represent logic 1 and logic 0. MIDI is a form of current loop system, and it operates in a manner more akin to switching a light bulb on and off than ordinary logic circuit methods. In fact the light bulb analogy is more accurate than you might think, since a MIDI output drives an opto-isolator at the receiving equipment. The opto-isolator consists of a light emitting diode (LED) with its light output aimed at a photocell. The LED and photocell are contained in an opaque case so that the only light the photocell can receive is that from the LED. Normally the photocell is switched off, but when the LED is activated, its light output causes the photocell device to switch on as well. A switching action is therefore transmitted through the device.

This may seem like a 'sledgehammer to crack a nut' sort of solution, but it has some definite advantages. The point of an opto-isolator is that it couples an electrical signal without using any direct electrical connection through the device. The most common reason for using a component of this type is when a high voltage in one item of equipment must not be coupled through to another piece of equipment. Although, on the face of it, there will be no high voltage to block in this application, this is not necessarily so. In most cases there will be no voltage to block, but with two pieces of equipment that are double insulated and do not have their chassis earthed, a substantial voltage difference can exist between the two chassis. Although a high voltage may be present, the power available is unlikely to be sufficient to present a hazard to anyone using the equipment. Many of the semiconductors in modern electronics are very vulnerable to damage by high voltages though, and could be damaged by any substantial voltage difference between the two chassis potentials. I must admit that I used to consider this a theoretical rather than actual risk. However, having done some rather expensive damage to a computer by not including an opto-isolator circuit, it is something I now take very much more seriously!

Another advantage of isolation is that in many systems the controlling equipment is a home computer or some other form of microcontroller. If there is one thing these do better than sequencing, it is producing electrical noise. Without the isolation this noise could be coupled into the instruments and would be heard as background buzzes and clicks on their audio output signals.

Another advantage of the electrical isolation, and possibly the most significant one for most users, is that it avoids problems with earth or hum loops. Anyone who has ever connected together a system having a few instruments, a mixer, an amplifier, etc., will probably have experienced the dreaded background hum of such a loop. The opto-isolation does not totally prevent hum loops, as these can still be produced via the audio interconnections. But it does at least prevent the MIDI connections from making the problem worse.

The right connections

The system of coupling signals through a MIDI system might be a slightly unusual one, but as far as actually wiring-up a system is concerned, things are very straightforward indeed. The standard MIDI connector is a 5 pin DIN type. Actually there are several types of 5 pin DIN connector, but the most common type is the 180 degree variety, and this is the type used for MIDI interconnections. MIDI equipment is always fitted with the sockets, and a lead fitted with two 5 way DIN

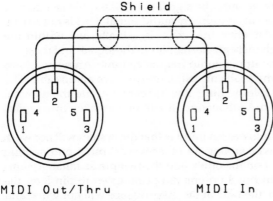

MIDI Out/Thru   MIDI In

Figure 1.9 Basic MIDI port interconnections

plugs is therefore needed to connect one piece of equipment to another. Fig. 1.9 shows the correct method of connection.

Although the connectors are 5 way types, MIDI requires only two interconnections, and three pins of each plug are left unused. Actually this is not quite true. Pins 4 and 5 are used to carry the signal, but pin 2 connects to the screen of the cable. A screened cable consists of one or more insulated leads having a sheath of braided wires, and then a layer of insulation over that. MIDI connecting cables are made from twin screened lead with the two inner connectors carrying the signal. The purpose of the outer connector is to screen the signal leads so that they do not radiate significant amounts of radio frequency interference. This is the opposite of the screened jack leads used to carry audio signals in electronic music systems. With these the screen is needed to prevent unwanted pick-up of electrical signals, rather than to prevent them from being radiated.

The shield is connected to pin 2 of both plugs, but MIDI equipment has only pin 2 connected to earth at sockets which send signals. Pin 2 is left unconnected at sockets which receive signals. This is essential, as otherwise the shield would connect the chassis of the two pieces of equipment together, making the opto-isolation pointless.

DIY cables

Anyone who is handy with a soldering iron should have little difficulty in wiring up their own leads, but ready-made MIDI leads are now readily available. If you do make your own, any twin screened cable should be suitable, even the thinner and cheaper varieties. I have seen the use of very high quality cable recommended on several occasions, apparently because the signal in a MIDI cable is at higher frequencies than those in an ordinary audio signal. This is not strictly accurate as the fundamental frequency is actually just within the audio range, although there are harmonics in the signal, and these extend well beyond the upper audio frequency limit. Anyway, I have never encountered any problems using inexpensive audio cable. The currents in a MIDI cable are quite low incidentally, and the nominal LED current is just 5 mA (about one-fiftieth of that taken by a typical torch bulb).

An important point to bear in mind is that the system will not work if the cable uses cross-coupling. In other words, pin 4 on one plug must connect to pin 4 on the other, and the two pin 5s must be similarly connected. With pin 4 on one plug connected to pin 5 on the other, and vice versa, the LED in the opto-isolator will not work, and the signal will not be coupled through the system. Some 5 way DIN leads intended for use with tape recorders and hi-fi systems do have cross-coupling, and are unsuitable for MIDI use.

A few manufacturers produce MIDI equipment that has the more durable (and expensive) XLR connectors instead of the DIN type. This type of connector is normally found only on equipment that is designed for use on the road where the DIN type might prove to be too fragile and unreliable. The pin numbering for connectors is shown in Fig. 1.10. The use of these connectors is within the MIDI specification, but only if the manufacturer produces suitable adapters to permit the equipment to be easily integrated into a setup which uses 5 pin DIN connectors.

There are three different types of MIDI socket; IN, OUT, and THRU. IN and OUT are self explanatory, and the OUT socket of the MIDI con-

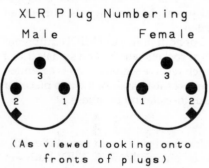

Figure 1.10 XLR connector pin numbering. Ready made leads and DIN adaptors should be available for MIDI equipment that uses these

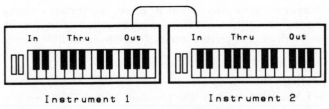

Instrument 1   Instrument 2

Figure 1.11 The basic master/slave interconnection

troller is coupled to the IN socket of whatever piece of equipment is being controlled. A very basic MIDI setup would just consist of one synthesizer connected to another, as shown in Fig. 1.11. This is the equivalent of the old system of using gate and CV connections to make one instrument act as a slave to the other. As we shall see later though, it is vastly more versatile.

There are almost endless permutations possible with MIDI equipment, but Fig. 1.12 shows a typical setup. This has a computer (or other micro-controller) as the basis of the system. Accordingly, the MIDI output socket of the computer connects through to the MIDI input socket on the first instrument. Most controllers allow music to be programmed by playing it on the keyboard of an instrument in the system. Therefore, the OUT socket on the first instrument is coupled to the IN socket of the controller so that note information can be read from the keyboard of this instrument. It clearly makes sense to have the instrument with the best keyboard as instrument 1.

Where several instruments must be driven from a single controller it is not advisable to make up a cable that simply wires all the inputs to the output of the controller. The MIDI system operates by switching a current of about 5 mA on and off. If two or three inputs are driven from a single output, the 5 mA current is shared between these inputs, quite possibly giving too little current to drive any of them properly.

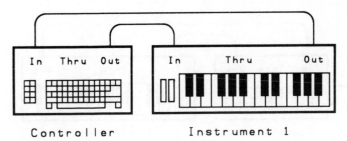

Controller   Instrument 1

Figure 1.12 The most basic setup for (external) real time sequencing

I have on occasions used one output to drive two inputs without encountering any difficulties, but this cannot be relied upon to work in every case. With more than two inputs driven from a single output there is very little chance of success.

THRU and THRU
The standard MIDI solution to this problem is the THRU socket, which is another output socket. However, its output signal is a replica of the signal received at the input socket, and is not a duplicate of the signal at the instrument's OUT socket. The THRU name is perhaps a little misleading in that it suggests that the signal at the input socket is simply coupled straight through to this socket. In fact the signal is coupled through to the THRU socket via a buffer amplifier so that the input receives the full 5 mA of current, and the THRU socket delivers the full 5 mA to the next instrument in the system. As Fig. 1.13 shows, the instruments are chained together, with the THRU socket of one being connected to the IN socket of the next.

Just how many instruments can be successfully connected together in this way is something that the MIDI specification does not mention. The accuracy of the signal must be degraded somewhat each time it passes through an instrument, and presumably there is a finite number of instruments that can be fitted into the system before the

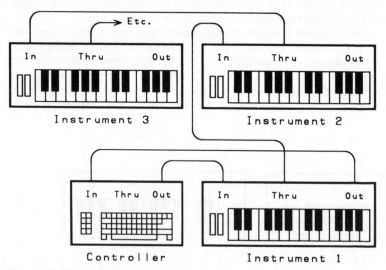

Figure 1.13 The 'chain' method of interconnection

signal is degraded to an unacceptable extent. The number of instruments that can be chained together is probably large enough to make it irrelevant to even the most lavishly equipped of us!

An objection to the chaining system that is sometimes put forward is that of the delays that are introduced. In my opinion at any rate, this problem is vastly over-stated. There is indeed a delay between a signal entering at the IN socket and exiting at the THRU socket. There is no reason why this should be more than a few microseconds though, and with a number of instruments connected together, the accumulated delay would still seem to be insignificant. When making checks on my MIDI equipment I have never been able to measure a significant delay.

What is a much more real problem with the chain system of connection is the lack of THRU sockets on many pieces of equipment. Something that always has to be kept in mind when dealing with MIDI systems is that the MIDI standard sets down what is a maximum specification and not a minimum one. The fact that something is described in the MIDI specification does not mean that all pieces of MIDI equipment will actually have it! The THRU socket is certainly part of the specification that is absent from many pieces of equipment, and I bought several pieces of MIDI gear before I obtained one which actually had a THRU socket. With a MIDI controller it is excusable to omit the THRU socket, as it is difficult to envisage a situation in which it would serve any useful purpose. With controlled equipment it is a more serious omission. If only one item of controlled equipment is to be used then there is obviously no problem. In a multi-instrument setup there is no problem if only one instrument lacks the THRU socket, as this instrument can be connected as the last one in the chain. If two or more instruments lack this facility then the chain method of connection is unusable.

Star system

The alternative to chaining equipment together is the so-called 'star' system. This uses an arrangement of the type shown in Fig. 1.14, but it requires an additional piece of hardware in the form of a 'THRU-box'. These are not particularly expensive to buy, and are quite simple pieces of electronics. Some people prefer this method to the chain system of connection. I use the star system merely because I have several pieces of equipment that lack a THRU socket, and I consequently have little alternative. I don't think I would bother with the complication of a THRU-box if I did have the choice.

In a complex setup it is possible that a THRU-box will provide too few THRU sockets. There should be no problem in using one THRU-

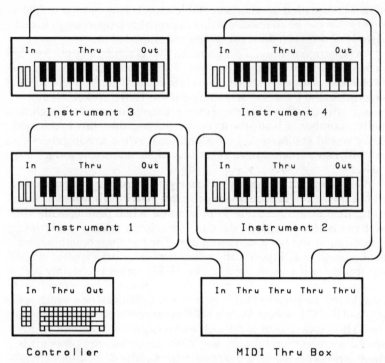

Figure 1.14 The 'star' method of connection (which here, and in practice, is usually far from star-like)

box to drive another in order to provide more outputs, or it is quite in order to use a mixture of star and chain connections, as shown in Fig. 1.15.

Possibilities of MIDI

A later chapter deals with the possibilities opened up by MIDI, and the types of system that can be put together. However, it would be helpful here to have a brief look at some of the things that can be achieved with the aid of MIDI.

At a most basic level an instrument can be used to control a second instrument in order to give thicker sounds. This is rather like connecting together two analogue synthesizers via their gate/CV sockets. The MIDI version is much more versatile though. In particular, MIDI can

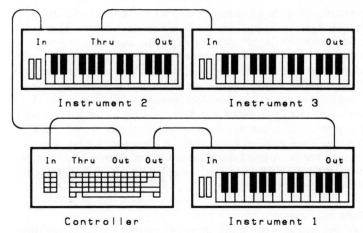

Figure 1.15 A combination of 'star' and 'chain' connection may sometimes be the easiest solution

handle polyphonic operation, and with suitable instruments split keyboard operation is possible. In other words, notes above a certain point on the keyboard produce one voice, while notes below that point produce another. By assigning the two voices to separate MIDI channels a suitable slave instrument will also play two different voices. With many instruments it is now possible to send voice information from one instrument to another.

Two interesting developments in MIDI equipment are the MIDI keyboard and the rack-mount instruments (expanders). A MIDI keyboard generates MIDI data when it is played, but it does not have any form of built-in sound generation circuit. A rack-mount instrument is generally a standard keyboard instrument with the keyboard omitted. It can be played only via the MIDI input socket. The main idea of these types of equipment is that they enable a system to be put together which has a single high quality keyboard. This avoids the expense of buying several keyboard instruments when they will be put together in a system which renders all but one of the keyboards irrelevant. It also gives a neater and more compact system.

Keyboardless instruments are not only suitable for use as slaves to keyboard instruments, they can also be used under computer control. A lot of musicians are less than enthusiastic about the use of computers in music, but a growing number of MIDI users are realizing the advantages and becoming converted to the idea. One of the earliest uses of computer control in music was in musical education. Systems which enable music to be entered on to an on-screen stave and then played by the computer have been available for some time. These represent what must be the ultimate musical learning tool.

The early systems used the computer's built-in sound generator to reproduce the music. This limited their application to educational and simple home entertainment purposes, since the sound quality of even the better computer sound generators generally falls somewhat short of good electronic instrument standards. Using a computer system which supports MIDI changes the situation radically, as any MIDI instrument can then be used instead of the computer's integral sound generation circuits. A good music notation program which includes MIDI support can be of tremendous value to composers and arrangers, whether amateur or professional.

Real time

Another popular music application of computers is in real-time sequencing. A notation program is an example of a step-time sequencer, where the music is programmed into the computer in some way, and then played back. Apart from educational use, a system of this type is of great advantage to those who have only limited playing ability, or to someone who is dealing with complex pieces of music that cannot be played by one person. A real-time sequencer is programmed by playing the music on the keyboard of a MIDI instrument, and the MIDI information from the keyboard is then stored in the computer's memory, together with timing information. This type of sequencer is primarily of interest to those who have plenty of playing ability, but are perhaps not very expert at musical theory. On the other hand, many real-time sequencers offer a facility to tidy up the timing of the playing if it is a little ragged!

Real-time sequencer programs often offer quite advanced features these days. Many are arranged like multi-track tape recorders, and even have tape recorder style controls such as play, record, rewind, etc. Also like a multi-track recorder, the music can be recorded one track at a time, gradually building up a complex piece of music. A system of this type can provide facilities that would be totally impracticable with conventional tape recording systems. These facilities are mainly concerned with editing, and many systems allow the music to be edited with what is really some form of step-time sequencer. Notes can be lengthened or shortened, or wrong notes can be changed to the right ones. If an instrument on one track does not sound quite right, another instrument can be assigned to that track. With many MIDI systems it is even possible to program instrument changes on each track. Using a MIDI sequencer to produce music is rather like using a word processor to produce a piece of text. With the word processor the idea is to get each piece of text just right before finally printing it out. With a sequencer the music is 'fine tuned' until it is just as required, and then it can be recorded for posterity using an ordinary stereo cassette recorder.

Most of the electronic instruments available today can produce a vast range of sounds, but this brings the drawback that setting the instrument up to produce each sound can require dozens of different parameters to be accurately set up. It can be time consuming to set up each voice of an instrument correctly, and it can be difficult for even the more technically minded users to find the right sounds in the first place. There are voice filer and other MIDI programs available for some combinations of computer and instrument, and these can greatly simplify setting and resetting the voice parameters.

A relatively recent development that is of great interest to many musicians is the low cost MIDI guitar. Guitarists have for many years been jealous of the vast and ever expanding range of sounds available to keyboard players, and there have been instruments in the past that incorporated synthesizer techniques. There have also been interfaces to enable electric guitars to be used with analogue synthesizers via their gate and CV sockets. The cost of such equipment has been quite high until recently, but with a MIDI equipped guitar and an inexpensive synthesizer the guitarist has a virtually limitless range of sounds available for what is a quite reasonable outlay.

There are obviously a lot of exciting possibilities with MIDI systems, but it would be all too easy to waste large sums of money on totally unsuitable equipment. It would also be quite simple to put together a very capable system, but to have great difficulty in getting it to do anything particularly worthwhile. In order to exploit MIDI a reasonable understanding of the subject is almost certainly essential.

2 Modes and channels

Before tackling MIDI codes it's a good idea to know a bit about MIDI modes and channels. The latter are quite simple in concept, and there are 16 of them numbered from 1 to 16. Having some form of channelling is important, since without it there is no way of directing information to one particular device in a system. The different modes govern how each piece of equipment handles the MIDI channels, and all the devices in a system do not necessarily have to be set to the same operating mode.

This may all seem like an unnecessary complication, and the various operating modes are perhaps an aspect of MIDI which has done much to cause confusion amongst new users. Changes in the names of the operating modes did not seem to help clarify matters either, and probably further increased the confusion. On the other hand, having several operating modes does increase the versatility of MIDI systems and equipment. More specifically, it enables MIDI to function well with any system from a basic two instrument setup to a highly complex computer controlled system. It enables simple instruments to be used effectively with more complex types, and it does not restrict the more sophisticated instruments to being used in one particular way.

In the mode

There are four standard MIDI operating modes which are numbered from 1 to 4, but they are also known by names such as 'omni' and 'mono'. A few manufacturers have introduced their own 'improved' operating modes, but all instruments should include at least one of the standard modes. Details of the four normal modes are provided here, and there's a quick reference chart in Appendix 1. Note that three names are given for each mode, and that these are respectively the mode number, the current mode name, and the previous mode name. The old names have been included as you are still likely to come across references to these from time to time. Mode 4 in particular, is still often referred to as the 'mono' mode. To my way of thinking neither the old nor the new names seem particularly apt or totally logical, and most people seem to use the mode numbers rather than the names these days.

Mode 1–Omni On/Poly (formerly Omni Mode)

This is the most basic operating mode, and a mode which every piece of MIDI equipment should support. This is normally the default mode (i.e. the one which devices adopt at switch-on). In this mode MIDI channel information is ignored and the equipment responds to information on any channel. The received note information is assigned to an instrument's voices polyphonically. In other words, in this mode an instrument tries to play every note that is received regardless of what channel it happens to be on. The exact way in which received information is assigned to the voices of the instrument depends on its design. A typical arrangement would be to have each received note played on the next available voice, with the instrument cycling through all its voices in sequence. Repeated notes are often assigned to the channel on which they were just played. On the instruments I have encountered the note information received via MIDI in mode 1 is handled in just the same way as it would be if the same notes were played on the keyboard (with the keyboard not set up for any form of split operation, of course).

In practice the exact method of note assignment is generally irrelevant, as in this mode the only way predictable results can be obtained is to have all voices set to produce the same sound. This mode was only ever envisaged as a very basic beginner's mode, and it is relatively foolproof in that with two instruments connected together and set to mode 1, anything played on the master instrument should be echoed by the slave instrument. This mode is relatively rather than completely foolproof in that it might not work properly if the master instrument has (say) 16 note polyphony while the slave instrument perhaps has only six note polyphony. If more notes are received at one time than there are voices to play them, obviously some notes will be missed out.

As instruments have become more sophisticated and MIDI users have gained experience, mode 1 has become much less used than it once was.

Mode 2–Omni On/Mono (No old name)

This mode is similar to mode 1, but received note information is handled monophonically rather than polyphonically. Note that the device will still respond to note information on any MIDI channel, but it will assign all notes to just one voice. This mode is intended for monophonic instruments, and if applied to a polyphonic type, the instrument is effectively down-graded to a monophonic instrument.

With only one note at a time possible, there is obviously a risk of too many notes at a time being received. Much more so than for a polyphonic instrument used in mode 1. There are three ways in which an excessive number of notes can be handled. Either the lowest, highest, or last note received can be played (you may have the choice of selecting whichever one of these you like).

As monophonic instruments are something of a dying breed, and there is no obvious reason for down-grading a polyphonic instrument to monophonic operation, this mode does not seem to be of great use to most MIDI users.

Mode 3–Omni Off/Poly (formerly Poly Mode)

The 'omni off' part of the name indicates that this mode is not one which responds to any channel. In fact it will ignore all note information that is not on a specific channel. As the 'poly' part of the name implies, this mode provides polyphonic operation. This gives much greater versatility than the previous two modes, but the system must be carefully set up so that the right channels are used by the transmitting device and the receiving instruments. If the sending and receiving devices are set to different channels, nothing will happen when the system is set in motion.

This is a useful mode in that it enables several instruments to be independently sequenced by a computer or other controlling device. Furthermore, polyphonic operation is possible on up to 16 channels. Unfortunately, in order to make the most of this mode you would need 16 polyphonic instruments!

Mode 4–Omni Off/Mono (formerly Mono Mode)

This is the mode which is widely regarded as the most powerful one, although I suppose that strictly speaking mode 3 offers the greatest scope. However, as pointed out previously, taking full advantage of mode 3, or anything approaching full advantage, would be an expensive business. Mode 4 offers great power and flexibility at much lower cost.

In mode 4 each voice of an instrument is assigned to a separate MIDI channel. Thus, with a 16 channel multi-timbral instrument that supports mode 4, or perhaps with two suitable eight channel instruments, it is possible to have 16 different sounds with each one sequenced independently. With one or two instruments in mode 4 you can have what is virtually a programmable orchestra. With mode 4, a base channel is assigned to the instrument, and then its voices occupy this and subsequent channels. For instance, if an eight voice instrument has channel 4 set as the base one, then its voices are assigned to channels 4 to 11.

Although mode 4 is certainly very powerful, there are some points which should be borne in mind if you are contemplating using it. First and foremost is that in the past relatively few instruments have supported this mode. More manufacturers seem to be admitting to its existence these days, but there are still some quite expensive MIDI equipped instruments available which simply do not have this mode. Also, unless an instrument can have a different sound assigned to each voice there would seem to be little point in using mode 4. If you have instruments that do support mode 4, read the MIDI section of their manuals very carefully to discover just how independent the voices of each instrument really are. I have SCI 'Six-Traks' synthesizers which will respond to pitch wheel modulation sent via MIDI, but this modulation applies to all channels regardless of which channel it is received on. Mode 4 permits the 16 channels to be controlled fully independently, but it is not a requirement of the MIDI standard that this should be the case.

As the mono part of the omni off/mono name indicates, each channel is only capable of monophonic operation. This will not necessarily matter, but mode 3 or a combination of modes 3 and 4 might offer better results in some cases. In Fig. 2.1, for the sake of simplicity we

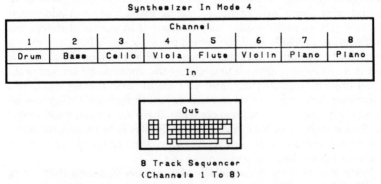

Figure 2.1 A single mono mode instrument can be very effective but lacks versatility

are assuming that eight tracks are available, and that we require a piano and six other sounds. Using a single synthesizer in mode 4 to provide these is a bit restricting in that only two channels are left for the piano sound, so that the piano can play no more than two notes at once. The arrangement of Fig. 2.2 is more versatile, but it requires two instruments. A synthesizer provides the six piece accompaniment, as before, but this time the piano sound is provided by a 16 note polyphonic electronic piano or synthesizer. This permits a full piano part to be produced without having to compromise on the accompaniment.

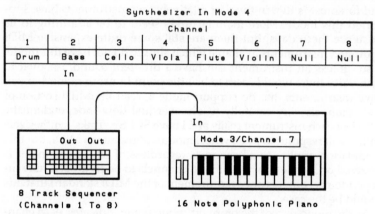

Synthesizer In Mode 4

Channel							
1	2	3	4	5	6	7	8
Drum	Bass	Cello	Viola	Flute	Violin	Null	Null

In

Out   Out

8 Track Sequencer
(Channels 1 To 8)

In

Mode 3/Channel 7

16 Note Polyphonic Piano

Figure 2.2 A combination of modes 3 and 4 can provide outstanding results

Variations

A large percentage of the more recent instruments go beyond mode 4, and offer some form of "multi" mode instead of or in addition to mode 4. These multi modes vary somewhat in points of detail, and you need to carefully read the "small print" in the MIDI implementation chart in order to find out precisely what facilities they offer. In fact it is sometimes difficult to decipher the appropriate section of the MIDI implementation chart, and you might need the assistance of a knowledgeable sales person in order to sort things out. Difficulties are most likely to occur in this respect when there are several multi modes to choose from. The basic idea of multi modes is to let an instrument effectively operate as two or more mode 3 instruments, or "virtual" instruments as they are sometimes called.

These modes vary principally in the number channels that can be used, and the number of notes per channel. Some are quite restrictive, with perhaps eight voices being split up on the basis two per channel on four channels, or four per channel on two channels. The more sophisticated instruments have dynamic voice allocation. In other words, an eight voice instrument could be used with (say) up to eight notes per channel on up to eight channels. This is not quite as good as it sounds, since the eight voices would limit the number of notes played at once to just eight. However, being able to use something like six notes on one channel and two on another, immediately followed by four notes on each of the two totally different channels, without the need for any mode changes, obviously extends the versatility of the instrument and its ease of use.

Obviously manufacturers are now trying very hard to improve the versatility of instruments for those who require (and can handle) complex systems. Fortunately, if this type of thing does not interest you, the instruments are still capable of operating in more basic ways. One of these more basic ways, and a very useful one, is with keyboard instruments that support split keyboard operation. This is where one half of the keyboard is assigned to certain voices of the instrument, while the other half is assigned to the remaining voices. The point of this is that it enables one sound to be played with the right hand while a different sound is used for the bass accompaniment played with the left hand. When applied to MIDI, the two sections of the keyboard can often be assigned to different channels. This enables a slave instrument to similarly use different sounds for the left and right hand parts.

Transmission

When an instrument is set to a MIDI reception mode, its sending mode is changed as well. In theory data can be sent on any channel in mode 1 or mode 2, but the convention is that the data is sent on the base channel. This can often be assigned to any realistic channel (you cannot have a base channel that would push the highest channel above the MIDI limit of 16), but otherwise it will be channel 1. Similarly, in mode 3 an instrument transmits data on the base channel. In mode 4 data will be sent on the same channels as those assigned to the voices for reception purposes. More or less what it boils down to is that when something is played on the keyboard, the transmitted data is the same as the data that would need to be received in order to mimic the keyboard playing.

Not all MIDI equipment actually has operating modes as such. What we are really talking about here are home computers plus MIDI software and some of the other forms of micro-controller. Which mode is effectively in force depends on how such a system is used, and its capabilities. Most micro-controllers will at least allow polyphonic operation on one channel, which corresponds to mode 3 operation. Many will permit monophonic sequencing on several channels, and possibly all 16 channels giving what is effectively mode 4 operation. Some will even permit multi-channel polyphonic sequencing, or a sort of multiple mode 3 operation.

Which mode?

It is important to understand the differences between MIDI modes as you must set each piece of equipment in the system to the right mode before everything will work as desired. Just how the mode is changed is something that varies from one instrument to another, and it is a matter of consulting the manuals in order to find out which combinations of buttons have to be pressed (or whatever). Things are relatively simple if you merely wish to connect one instrument to act as the slave to another. Mode 1 will probably suffice, and both instruments should default to this mode at switch-on. Incidentally, it is perfectly all right to cross couple the IN and OUT sockets of the two instruments, as in Fig. 2.3. Playing on either keyboard should then play both instruments. What you must never do is complete the loop with the chain method of connection, as shown in Fig. 2.4. In theory any data transmitted by the controlling instrument will be circulated around the system indefinitely. It might not work out quite like this in practice, but the system might not function properly anyway.

Mode 1 is fine if each instrument is required to produce only one sound, and all the instruments must play in unison, but for multi-timbral operation mode 3 or mode 4 is required. Which one to use is a matter of whether or not a channel will be used polyphonically. If more than one note at a time must be played by a channel, then that one at least must be in mode 3. As already explained, mode 3 is fine if

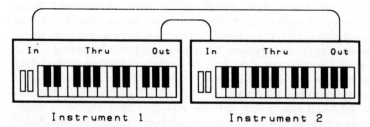

Figure 2.3 This method of cross-coupling is acceptable (playing either keyboard plays both instruments)

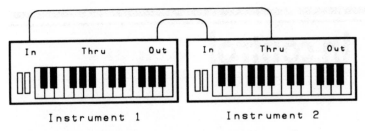

Instrument 1   Instrument 2

Figure 2.4 This looped method of 'chain' connection will not work

money is no object, but it is not practicable for most of us to have one instrument per channel.

Multi-timbral arrangements

A multi-timbral instrument with mode 4, perhaps augmented by another instrument in mode 3 or mode 4, is a much more affordable solution. Better still, a couple of instruments that can implement a multi mode with dynamic channel allocation will probably be limited only by your imagination, not by their music making capabilities. If you intend to use mode 3, mode 4 or a multi mode (or any combination of these), one point I cannot stress hard enough is the importance of finding out just what your instruments can achieve in these modes. Some (particularly older instruments) lack mode 4 and (or) a multi mode, while others have mode 4 plus a choice of sophisticated multi modes that enable you to fully exploit the instrument's voices. In general, an instrument intended for operation with a sequencer is likely to support more sophisticated MIDI control than one that is primarily a keyboard instrument.

Sequencers vary enormously in the degree of sophistication they offer. I do not know of any that restrict the user to simple mode 1 or mode 2 operation, but I do not know of any that permit 16 note polyphony on 16 channels either. There is clearly no point in buying a lot of sophisticated hardware that the sequencer will not be able to properly exploit. If you are going to use any form of sequencer a great deal, then instruments that support mode 3 and mode 4 are virtually essential.

If you are one of the growing band of MIDI guitarists, then mode 4 has its advantages. In theory mode 1 should be perfectly all right for guitar use, but in practice mode 4 with completely separate control of each channel often gives better results by avoiding unwanted and unpredictable effects with pitch bend etc.

3 In control

The importance of understanding the MIDI control code language is something that depends on how deeply involved with MIDI you intend to become. If you wish to do no more than twin two synthesizers via their MIDI sockets, knowing anything about the method of coding is probably of no value at all. If, on the other hand, you wish to produce computer software for use with MIDI systems, a highly detailed knowledge of the subject is certainly essential. I would guess that most of us fall somewhere between these two extremes, and that we require a basic understanding of the full range of codes. Without such an understanding you will not know what can and what cannot be achieved via a MIDI interface. Also, the versatility of MIDI coding has an attendant problem in that different instruments will sometimes interpret the same messages in different ways. Also, some messages will be meaningless to most instruments and will be ignored. If you are going to use any fairly sophisticated MIDI system it is essential to have a reasonable understanding of the MIDI control language, otherwise you are likely to miss out on useful facilities that can be implemented with your system, or to waste time trying to implement functions that are not catered for.

In this chapter we will first consider the MIDI codes without going into great detail about the particular code numbers used, and this information is all that most readers will require. This is followed by in-depth coverage of the subject, including the sort of detailed information that MIDI software programmers will require. The second section is non-essential reading, but the more enquiring readers may like to go through it out of academic interest anyway. It provides an insight into the way in which many items of electronics are computer controlled via a serial interface. This second section also includes a number of tables that are useful for reference purposes.

MIDI specification

One important point to understand right from the start is that the MIDI specification sets down a framework within which equipment manufacturers must work, and not a minimum implementation which all instruments must meet.

Accordingly, the fact that a piece of equipment has MIDI sockets does not mean that it will make use of all the codes and facilities described here. In fact I doubt if there has ever been a MIDI instrument that does exploit every MIDI code. There is no minimum specification which a piece of equipment must reach before its manufacturer is entitled to use the MIDI name. I suppose that something as basic as a percussion synthesizer which only responded to note on and note off information could be justifiably described as a MIDI equipped instrument.

What this means to users is that they have to study equipment manuals in order to find out just what parts of the MIDI standard are actually implemented.

Another point to bear in mind is that MIDI was designed to be able to incorporate developments in instrument technology. This means that some instruments may have facilities that go beyond the standard specification, although they should have standard modes that enable them to function properly with normal MIDI equipment. It is again a matter of checking through manuals to see if any items of your equipment have any useful 'frills'.

The exact method of setting MIDI modes, base channels, and certain other parameters is something else that has to be carefully gleaned from manuals. Parameters of this type can often be set via the MIDI input, but only if you have some means of generating the right codes. The right equipment and software will often be lacking, and the controls of the instruments will then have to be used. Instruments will normally respond to note on/off information without any need to activate the MIDI input via the controls. This is not true of all MIDI codes though, and things like filter resonance settings and envelope parameters are usually only accepted once they have been activated by the appropriate control settings. Unfortunately, with many instruments a few buttons and simple displays are used to control vast numbers of functions, and some odd combinations of key presses can be needed in order to set MIDI parameters.

MIDI messages consist of a status byte followed (usually) by a data byte or bytes. Unlike some digital control systems, MIDI does not use a fixed number of bytes in each message. The fixed format method has its advantages, but it often results in large numbers of dummy bytes when simple messages are being sent. This is undesirable with MIDI where it could slow down the sending of data to an unacceptable level. To avoid confusion all MIDI status bytes have the most significant bit set to 1, while data bytes always have this bit set to 0.

Channel voice messages

There are several categories of MIDI message, but we will start with the channel voice messages which are the ones of greatest importance to most users. These are codes which control the voices of an instrument, and are responsible for switching notes on and off, handling the keyboard velocity, pitch bend, etc.

Note on

The obvious starting point is the 'note on' message. The first byte is the 'note on' status byte, but only the four most significant bits are used for the 'note on' coding and to indicate that the byte is a status type. The four least significant bits contain the channel number. Where a byte is divided into two four bit sections in this way, each half (believe it or not) is termed a 'nibble'. With four bits available for the channel number, in terms of the equivalent decimal numbers, a range of 0 to 15 is available. As mentioned previously, MIDI channels are normally numbered from 1 to 16, but this discrepancy between the identification numbers and the actual values used to select them is something that need concern only MIDI software writers.

Note that all MIDI channel voice messages have a status byte where the most significant nibble carries the message type, and the least significant nibble bears the channel number. The most significant bit of a status byte is always set to 1, while the most significant bit of a data byte is always 0. Although, on the face of it, there is no danger of status and data bytes being confused by equipment, as we shall see shortly, under certain circumstances one MIDI message can be mixed into another one. This simple method of differentiating the two types of byte ensures that equipment can sort things out correctly.

Note value

There are three bytes in a note on message, and the second one carries the note value. With the most significant bit set to 0 to indicate that the byte is a data type, this gives only seven bits to carry the note value. When converted from binary to decimal this equates to a range of values from 0 to 127. A value of 60 gives middle C, and each increment by one raises the note by one semitone. This gives a vast compass of around ten and a half octaves, which should be more than sufficient for any requirements.

However, once again it is a case of MIDI being able to accommodate a certain level of performance without all MIDI equipped instruments necessarily being able to take full advantage of it. Most instruments fall some way short of having the full 127 note range. Rather than simply ignoring notes outside their compass, most instruments seem to play the same note in the nearest octave that is within their range. From the musical viewpoint, this minimizes the effect of out of range notes being programmed. The range of notes that can be sent will normally be determined by an instrument's keyboard, although the ranges of notes can often be extended by switching all the notes up or down by one octave.

It is not uncommon for an instrument to be capable of receiving a wider range of notes than can be transmitted. This means that some instruments can achieve a wider range of notes via the MIDI input than can be played via their keyboards. The difference can be a couple of octaves or more. Playing an instrument via an external MIDI keyboard (or via the larger keyboard of another instrument) will often give an increased compass, but some form of sequencer may be the only way of obtaining the full range of notes. This sort of thing is nothing new incidentally, and some analogue synthesizers can accommodate about 10 octaves via their CV inputs, but can only handle around half this when played using their keyboards. With both types of instrument the manual or a specification sheet should clearly show the available range of notes under external control.

Velocity

The third byte in the note on sequence provides keyboard velocity information. The range of available values is again 0 to 127. 0 represents minimum velocity, running through to maximum velocity at a value of 127. Keyboard velocity is determined by measuring the time taken for the key to be moved from its 'up' position to the 'down' position. This parameter is normally used to control the volume of notes. The harder you play the keyboard the louder the notes, as is the case with pianos and many acoustic keyboard instruments. The MIDI specification does not state that there must be some precise relationship between velocity value and output level, but there is probably no great variation from one instrument to another.

One obvious problem with the velocity value is that far from all instruments have velocity sensitive keyboards. Not all those that do are capable of transmitting velocity information on their MIDI outputs.

Even where no velocity information is available, a velocity value must be transmitted. The standard solution to this problem is for a middle value of 64 to be used. The velocity byte must always be transmitted as the receiving equipment will be expecting it to be present. A sensible value must be used in order to maintain reasonable compatibility with instruments that will respond to this information.

Note off

Once a note has been switched on it can only be switched off again by a suitable MIDI message. The system does not operate by having timing information coded into note on command to indicate note duration (which would be all right for sequencing, but difficult to apply to live performances). The MIDI standard provides two normal methods of switching notes off, and one of these is to use a note on instruction with a velocity value of 0. This is not the standard method, but quite a number of instruments do transmit note off messages in this form these days. The standard note off message is one having the appropriate status byte. This instruction takes exactly the same general form as the note on message, with the status byte also containing the channel number, and the next two bytes carrying note and velocity values.

At first sight there may seem to be no point in putting all this information into the note off instruction. What has to be kept in mind is that MIDI can handle several notes at once on each channel, and can have several channels being simultaneously sequenced. The note off instruction must therefore make it perfectly clear which particular note on which channel must be turned off. Some instruments can use the velocity information generated as a key is released to control the release phase of the envelope shaper. In many cases this feature will not be implemented, and then a dummy value will be inserted here.

With the note off message it is not necessary for the status byte to be sent every time. I have not encountered a system which actually seems to use this method, but presumably one note off status byte followed by a series of note and velocity values will turn off several notes, and would certainly contain fewer bytes than a series of individual messages.

Program change

This is an instruction that does not seem particularly exciting at first, but it can greatly enhance the capabilities of a simple MIDI sequencer system. Most instruments have a number of preset or preprogrammed sounds, or 'programs' as they are often termed. With some instruments only one of these programs can be used at one time, but with others it is possible to assign a different program to each voice. The MIDI program change message enables the program used by an instrument, or a particular voice of an instrument, to be changed mid-piece. This can be useful when a slave instrument must follow program changes on the master, but it perhaps has most potential when applied to sequencing.

If an eight channel instrument which supports mode 4 is being sequenced, on the face of it there are only eight different sounds available. If the instrument has a hundred programs stored internally and ready for use, then via the program change instruction it is possible to set any channel to any desired program. This effectively gives a choice of one hundred sounds, not eight. Of course, a maximum of eight instruments can be used at once, but this system still gives greatly enhanced versatility. If you were writing a piece for string and brass instruments, but at some point you wished to introduce a different instrument such as a flute, provided one channel of the system is otherwise unused, it can be switched to a flute sound, and then switched back again once the flute part has been completed.

Remember that MIDI is restricted to 16 channels. Even if you could afford dozens of synthesizers to give a few hundred different sounds, there would be far too few MIDI channels to accommodate them. This system saves money and enables a wide range of sounds to be sequenced, albeit with a lot of hopping from one program to another in some cases. Most of the more sophisticated sequencer software can handle program changing.

An important point to realize is that there is no standardization of MIDI program sounds. Program number 10 might be a piano on one instrument, a flute on another, and a purely electronic sound on a third instrument. With only 128 program numbers available it would not really be practicable to have standard sounds anyway, since the range of available sounds is far too wide to be fitted into such a small range of values. The best that could be achieved would be to have standardized broad categories of sound. Even this would not be fool-proof, as many instruments enable the user to set up any program to give any available sound.

What this all means in practice is that you have to make quite sure that the instruments are set up with the right sound assigned to each program number that will be used. You may be satisfied with a standard range of sounds that are programmed into the instrument each time it is used. If this is too restrictive, some sort of chart will probably have to be drawn up for each sequence, showing which sounds should be assigned to which program numbers. The system will still work if mistakes are made in the program assignments, but you will end up with something like a violin playing the trumpet part! Some form of computerized sound filing and retrieval system can make the assigning of the right sound to the right program number much easier.

Although the number of programs supported by MIDI is 128, not all instruments support program changing, and of those that do not all implement the full range. The program change instruction is a two byte type, with the first byte carrying the program change code plus the channel number. The next byte is the value to select the required program number.

This value is from 0 to 127, but the programs are sometimes numbered from 1 to 128. However, there are exceptions, and with some instruments programs are organized in groups. The numbering may then be sets of two digit codes, or some other system which is nothing like the 1 to 128 type. Unlike the MIDI channel values, this is not something that is only of academic importance. Some reading of manuals or experimentation with the equipment may be needed to ascertain which program is selected by a particular program number sent from a sequencer.

Pitch bend

The basic MIDI note control instructions only permit the use of perfect semitones, but pitch bending is possible via a separate command. This command consists of three bytes, and the first of these is the appropriate command byte complete with the channel number. The next two are data bytes, and the seven usable bits of each one are combined to produce a 14 bit binary number. The first byte contains the least significant bits, while the second byte contains the seven most significant bits. In terms of equivalent decimal numbers this gives a range from 0 to 16384, which gives extremely fine pitch control.

In fact the degree of pitch control is much higher than is really justified, and there is a potential problem with this method. For this level of resolution to be worthwhile the pitch must be varied in quite small increments, but this requires a large number of messages to be sent within quite a short period of time. The speed of MIDI is such that it can barely accommodate high resolution pitch bend on one channel, let alone multi-channel pitch bending mixed in with other messages.

In practice seven bit resolution should be sufficient to provide smooth pitch variations with no apparent stepping.

Apparently many instruments only implement seven bit resolution, with a dummy byte (having a value of zero) being used for the least significant byte. Not all equipment falls into this class though, and my SCI equipment transmits and recognizes full 14 bit values. Whichever method is used, zero pitch bend is given with the most significant byte at 64, and the least significant byte at zero. This equates to a decimal value of 8192. The MIDI specification does not stipulate a specific relationship between pitch bend values and the degree of bend provided, and there are probably significant variations from one instrument to another. A variation of at least plus and minus one semitone would normally be possible, and typically a much greater range would be possible. With some instruments pitch bend information is recognized only if this facility is enabled via the instrument's controls. This gives the option of having a slave instrument ignore pitch bending data from the master instrument.

Control change

A brief look at an analogue synthesizer leaves an impression of an instrument that is 95% controls and 5% keyboard. Modern instruments may seem to be lacking in controls by comparison, but in most cases there are far more controls on modern digital instruments than on their analogue predecessors. The lack of knobs and switches is due to modern electronics being used to enable a few physical controls to provide a multitude of electronic adjustments. A typical arrangement would have a keypad to select the number of the desired parameter (filter resonance, envelope amount, etc), and then a control knob and digital display to enable the required level to be set. One control knob, a keypad, and a simple display can replace literally hundreds of knobs and switches.

Control numbers

For maximum versatility MIDI must provide access to these parameters so that they can be altered by a sequencer or other MIDI controller. This access can be provided via the MIDI controller message, which is another three byte type. The message is in the usual format, with the first byte carrying the control change code and the channel number. The next two bytes are data bytes, with the first of these giving the identification number for the control that is to be altered, and the next one giving the new value. This is actually a slight over-simplification, as there are not 128 different controls available with each one having a data range of 0 to 127. This would be a nice, simple scheme of things, but it does not take into account the fact that not all controls are of the variable type. Some are switches that only require a basic on/off action. Also, for some purposes the resolution provided by seven bit control might not be enough.

Consequently, some MIDI controls are allocated to on/off switching, while others are paired so that they can be used together to provide 14 bit resolution. Some have been left undefined. The latter are the controller values from 96 to 120, and the 'switches' are controls from 64 to 95. A value of 0 sets a 'switch' off, and a value of 127 turns it on. Values other than 0 and 127 should not be used, and could have an unpredictable result, although they should simply be ignored by all MIDI equipment.

High resolution

Controllers from 0 to 63 are the variable controllers. However, they are organized into two groups of 32, with one group providing the most significant bytes and the other providing the least significant bytes. Consequently, values from 0 to 63 only provide 32 controllers, but with 14 bit resolution. This table helps to explain the way in which things are organized.

Controller	MSB control no.	LSB control no.
0	0	32
1	1	33
2	2	34
....		
29	29	61
30	30	62
31	31	63

When the setting of a variable controller must be altered, it is not necessary to alter both data bytes if only one actually needs to be changed in order to set the new value. It is not even necessary to implement both bytes if the application does not warrant more than seven bit resolution. For seven bit operation the least significant byte is the one that is not implemented.

There is a body of opinion which feels that the high resolution controller mode is impracticable. As pointed out in the section dealing with pitch bend, there can be a problem in transmitting data fast enough to exploit 14 bit resolution properly. There is little point in having thousands of different settings available, but then incrementing and decrementing controls in jumps of around a hundred. Ideally controllers would be stepped up and down in single unit steps, but with thousands of different settings available, and MIDI only being capable of handling about three thousand bytes per second, this might not always be feasible.

In fact matters are worse with the MIDI controllers than with the pitch bend message. The pitch bend message sends the 14 bits of data in a single three byte instruction. Due to the need to include the number of the controller to be altered, this cannot be achieved with the controllers. It could be achieved with a four byte instruction, but this method (with both data bytes in the same group) is not supported by MIDI. Instead, two three byte groups are required. This may seem an inefficient way of tackling things, but remember that there is no need to send the most significant byte unless this byte actually needs to be changed. When varying the 14 bit value in small increments, the most significant byte would only need to be changed perhaps once for every 64 changes of the least significant byte. This system is therefore only marginally less efficient than the pitch bend system, and is somewhat more efficient than using a four byte group.

A definite drawback of using this method of 14 bit resolution is that when both bytes must be altered, they cannot be changed simultaneously. This is also true with the pitch bend method of obtaining high resolution, but the delay between one byte and the next being received is very small as they are both in the same MIDI message. With the system used for the controllers the bytes are sent in separate messages, and there is a longer (although still quite short) delay. This delay could cause problems with audible glitches. This problem is not insurmountable, and the equipment could be designed to avoid it. In practice though, most equipment that makes use of the MIDI variable controllers only seems to use seven bit resolution. Actually, in some cases the least significant bit or bits are ignored, and the equipment only uses five or six bit resolution

Which control?

The obvious question now, is what does each MIDI controller actually control? The original MIDI specification had controller 0 as the pitch bender, but this is now assigned to its own channel message (as described previously). Controller 1 is the modulation wheel, but the others are not assigned to any specific tasks. There are conventions rather than standards for the use of the controllers, and no one is bound by these conventions. Manufacturers are free to use them in any way they like. This list gives the conventional controller assignments, which seem to have been heavily influenced by the popularity of the Yamaha DX7.

MIDI controller numbers

Control number	Function
1	Modulation wheel
2	Breath controller
4	Foot pedal
5	Portamento time
6	Data entry knob
7	Main volume control
64	Sustain pedal
65	Portamento
66	Sustenuto
67	Soft pedal
96	Data entry (increment)
97	Data entry (decrement)

Obviously most of the controls are not assigned to anything under this convention, which leaves plenty of scope for using them in any special functions. Bear in mind that MIDI receiving equipment does not necessarily mean an instrument of some kind. MIDI equipment includes such things as audio mixers and effects units, both of which can be controlled via MIDI control change messages. Much of MIDI's power and versatility lies in the control change message. While the conventions detailed above give a very basic level of compatibility between different pieces of equipment that use this facility, in general it is necessary for controlling software to be tailored to suit each instrument, effects units, or whatever. Some software has provision for customization to suit any piece of equipment within reason.

Assignable controls

A similar approach is used with some instruments, where any controller can be assigned to any MIDI controllable feature. This enables instruments to be set up for compatibility with controlling software, or with other instruments. If you have two MIDI instruments, one with preset control assignments and the other assignable controls, the latter can be set up for compatibility with the former. Assignable MIDI controls is certainly a very useful feature which greatly increases the chances of being able to exploit this facet of MIDI. It does not necessarily give total compatibility though. The fact that (say) control number 15 is used to control the filter cut off frequency on two instruments does not mean that given values will have precisely the same effect on both instruments. Although there is no standardization on this type of thing, discrepancies will in most cases be quite small. However, do not assume that this will always be the case, as there are always exceptions.

Some instruments respond to controller information only if they are set to the correct mode via the front panel controls, or by way of a system exclusive message (these are described later in this chapter). This facility can be used to prevent a slave instrument from responding to information from the master if it is not required to do so. As the slave will normally be set to produce different sounds to the master, and it might be a totally different instrument with different controller assignments anyway, this is a useful feature.

Mode changing

You may have noticed that no details have been provided for MIDI controls having numbers from 121 to 127. These are reserved for channel mode messages, and this mainly means changing MIDI mode via the MIDI interface (changing from default mode 1 to mode 4 for example). There are a couple of additional messages though. This table details the function of control numbers 121 to 127.

Channel mode message numbers

Control number	Function	Data
121	Reset all controls	Always 0
122	Local control	0 = off, 127 = on
123	All notes off	Always 0
124	Omni mode off	Always 0
125	Omni mode on	Always 0
126	Mono mode on	Number of channels
127	Poly mode on	Always 0

Local control

The reset all controls message simply sets all the MIDI controls back to their default settings (i.e. whatever settings they normally assume at switch-on). The mode change instruction retains the three byte format of the normal control change instruction, but in most cases the last byte is always zero and does not carry any information. One exception is the 'local control' instruction, where the third byte is either 0 to 127 to give on/off switching in the usual manner. Local control is a rather fancy term for what normally means the keyboard, although I suppose that any form of manual input to play an instrument is covered by this term (including a modulation wheel). This message obviously does not apply to instruments which do not have a keyboard or other means of local control. With local control switched on, the instrument functions normally, and this is the default mode. With local control disabled, playing the keyboard has no effect on the instrument, and it can only be played via the MIDI input socket. Note though, that the keyboard is still operational, and that anything played on it will generate the appropriate output signals from the MIDI output socket. In other words, an instrument that has a built-in keyboard is effectively turned into a MIDI expander and a separate keyboard.

This might not seem to be a particularly valuable feature, but it does have its uses. The most obvious one is to ensure that accidental manual operation (e.g. leaning on the keyboard) does not interfere with an instrument while it is being controlled by a sequencer. Another possibility is to take the output from the keyboard, feed it through some form of processor (such as a MIDI arpeggiator), and then feed it back into the instrument (Fig. 3.1). In this way it is possible to effectively

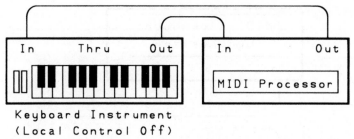

Keyboard Instrument
(Local Control Off)

Figure 3.1 A simple application of separating the keyboard and sound generator circuits

add features to an instrument, although as yet there are only limited possibilities.

Another use of this feature is when using a sequencer with a keyboard instrument and a rack-mount instrument. With real-time sequencing it is usually possible to play back a recorded sequence, and to dub a new track or tracks onto it (the MIDI equivalent of multi-track recording). Normally a setup of the type shown in Fig. 3.2 would be used, but this does not allow the new tracks to be played on the expansion module while the sequencer plays the existing tracks on the keyboard instrument. This can be achieved using the arrangement

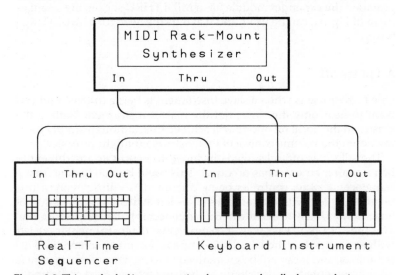

Figure 3.2 This method of interconnection does not work well when producing multi track real time sequences

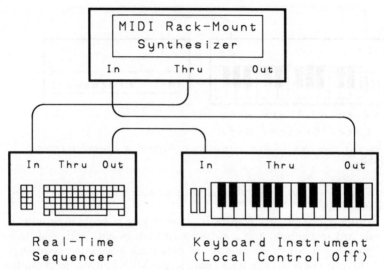

Real-Time   Keyboard Instrument
Sequencer   (Local Control Off)

Figure 3.3 This setup could be more appropriate to real time sequencing

shown in Fig. 3.3. This is not the only way of obtaining the desired
effect, and it could be achieved with the setup of Fig. 3.4. However,
provided the expander module has a MIDI THRU socket, the arrangement of Fig. 3.3 can be used, and it avoids the need for a MIDI THRU-
box.

All notes off

One further use is when a slave instrument is being utilized and you
want to hear only the slave, not the master instrument. Setting the
master to the 'local off' mode will achieve this, although simply turn-
ing down the volume control of this instrument might be easier!

The 'all notes off' message is included to permit an instrument to
be reset after an error has occurred. This could be due to data from a
sequencer or other controller being corrupted, resulting in an instrument being left with one or more notes left switched on. This sort of
error is most likely to occur when a sequencer is halted mid-sequence.
This message is an easy way of ensuring that the instrument is not left
with any notes switched on. This feature is not implemented in all instruments, and it can not be guaranteed to work. Where this feature is
not implemented, switching off an instrument and then switching it
on again will do the trick, although this takes it back to its start-up

condition and data (sound samples, program settings, etc.) might be lost. An alternative which is often effective is to use the keyboard to simultaneously play at least as many keys as the instrument has voices. Most instruments have a system of voice assignment that results in previous notes being terminated and new ones played instead when the instrument runs out of voices. Thus, when the keys are released, all notes should switch off.

Selecting the required MIDI mode can look a little confusing at first, but things are much easier if you use the new MIDI mode names rather than the old ones or the mode numbers (e.g. omni off/mono instead of mono mode or mode 4). Taking mode 4 as an example of how to select a desired mode, a message to controller 124 would switch the omni mode off, and a message to controller 126 would switch the mono mode on. There is a slight complication in that the second data byte for controller 126 (mono mode on) is not just a dummy value of zero. Instead, it indicates the number of channels that are to be allocated to mono operation. If, for example, eight channels are allocated, and the base channel has been set at 2, channels 2 to 9 will be allocated to mono operation. If a value of 0 is used, the instrument assigns all its available voices to mode 4 operation.

Not every instrument has all four MIDI modes available. Mode 4 is one that is often absent, and few instruments have mode 2

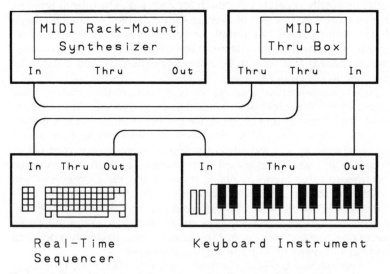

Figure 3.4 This achieves much the same result as the setup of Figure 3.3

implemented. Another point to keep in mind is that some instruments have a fixed base channel, and many only recognize a data value of zero when switching to mode 4. In other words, only all channels or none can be assigned to mode 4 operation. One final point is that all notes are switched off when there is a changed mode, although in practice it is unlikely that there would be any notes left to switch on anyway.

Aftertouch

Aftertouch is something that has only recently become implemented to a significant extent, with most instruments previously having only velocity sensitivity, or even just having a totally expressionless on/off keyboard action. Instruments which have aftertouch respond to the pressure on each key, as opposed to velocity sensitive types where it is the speed with which each key is depressed that the instrument reacts to. It is not a matter of only being able to have one or the other, and it would be quite feasible to have an arrangement where the velocity sets the initial volume of each note, and the aftertouch affects the volume and the filtering thereafter.

MIDI supports two types of aftertouch; the 'polyphonic' and the 'overall' varieties. The polyphonic type is the more sophisticated as it provides totally separate aftertouch for each key. The overall type, as its name implies, is a sort of average figure derived from all the keys that are being played. Polyphonic key pressure is a very desirable feature, but it is one that is available on few instruments. It requires complex keyboards that tend to be extremely expensive and difficult to maintain in full working order.

Those whose main interest is computer control rather than keyboard playing might be interested to know that velocity and aftertouch are not strictly for keyboard players. For example, some notation programs allow the use of standard dynamic notation (pp, ff, etc.), and will send velocity and (possibly) aftertouch information to control the dynamics of suitably endowed instruments. There are a number of rack-mount instruments available that can only be played via their MIDI input sockets, and which are mainly intended for computer controlled applications. A lot of these seem to respond to velocity information and aftertouch of one type or the other. This is perhaps not surprising, as most rack-mount instruments are effectively a popular keyboard instrument with the keyboard omitted!

The polyphonic key pressure message is a standard three byte type, with the first one containing the channel number and the polyphonic key pressure header code. This is followed by two data bytes with the first one indicating the note (or key if you prefer) that the pressure information relates to, and the second carrying the pressure value. The latter is from 0 to 127, with 0 corresponding to minimum pressure and 127 representing maximum pressure.

Only two bytes are needed for the overall key pressure message, since it does not have to indicate a particular note. It is therefore much the same as the polyphonic key pressure instruction, but with the appropriate header code in the first byte, and the middle byte omitted.

System common messages

This completes the description of the channel mode messages, and we will now move onto system messages. These differ from channel messages in that they are not sent to a particular channel, note, or controller, but are sent to the system as a whole. Messages in this category include song selection, drum machine timing, and system exclusive types. With no channel information being required, the first byte in an instruction does not carry a channel number. This leaves the least significant nibble free to carry other information, with the most significant nibble having the system common header code.

System exclusive

One of the main aims of MIDI was to provide built-out obsolescence, and it needed to have a large amount of built-in flexibility in order to stand any chance of achieving this. MIDI controllers give a great deal of flexibility, but they are inadequate for many purposes. In particular, most modern instruments deal in vast amounts of data, and the basic MIDI system provides no means of exchanging this between instruments. The system exclusive message uses two of the 16 codes available in the least significant nibble of the initial byte. One indicates that the system exclusive mode has been entered, and the other indicates that the system should return to normal MIDI operation.

Versatility
The system exclusive message provides tremendous versatility, as there is little restriction on what goes between the byte which switches equipment to the system exclusive mode, and the byte that returns the system to normal operation. In terms of the number of bytes that can be used, there is no upper limit at all! The only stipulation is that the first data byte must be the manufacturer's unique

identification number. It is this that gives the exclusive part of the system exclusive name. The idea of this is to enable manufacturers to implement any special features they like, which can not be accommodated by standard MIDI messages. The manufacturer's identification number is used as a key to gain access to any special features. This is perhaps looking at things the wrong way round, as the identification number is really used as a barrier to prevent an instrument from one manufacturer responding to system exclusive data from another manufacturer's equipment. There is no compatibility between the system exclusive data formats of various manufacturers, and the blocking process is essential if malfunctions are to be avoided when system exclusive messages are used in a system where the equipment is not all from a single manufacturer.

System exclusive messages may seem to go against one of the main concepts of MIDI, which was the idea of a truly standardized system. This is undeniably the case, but to be viable MIDI had to offer sufficient scope to let equipment manufacturers do their own thing. There would have been no point in devising a fully standardized system that was so restrictive that all the big names in the electronic music business refused to adopt it.

Virtually anything can be handled by system exclusive messages, and in some cases quite simple features are implemented via this feature. As an example, on the SCI Six Traks one of its functions is to enable and disable the double mode (an SCI mode which enables a slave Six Traks to precisely mimic a master instrument of the same type). Its main use is for features that require vast amounts of data to be swapped between pieces of equipment. A typical application would be where an instrument has (say) 100 programs, and the factory presets can be altered by the user. With most instruments the new settings will be lost when the instrument is switched off, and must be reset each time it is used. By means of system exclusive messages it would be possible to send all 100 modified programs to a computer where they could be stored on disk or tape, and quickly reloaded each time the instrument was used. The possibilities go beyond this simple scheme of things, and it is possible to have a library of programs so that the required sounds can be chosen and loaded into the instrument. A similar system can be applied to sound samples for sampling instruments.

Song select

This message has similarities to the program select instruction, and it is a two byte type which consists of the status byte followed by a data byte. This seven bit data byte enables one of 128 songs to be selected (numbered from 0 to 127). The song select message might more accurately be called sequence select, as it is used with a sequencer that can store a number of sequences, to call up the one that is required. A lot of instruments have built-in sequencers, and this message would be more likely to be used with one of these than a computer based sequencer (which generally issues commands rather than receives them). This message could be issued from a computer based MIDI control system to call up the required song on a drum machine for example.

Song pointer

The basic concept of this message is to set two sequencers to the same point in a song when starting somewhere other than at the beginning of a sequence. This is accomplished by having a counter circuit in MIDI sequencers that counts the number of beats. This only works up to a maximum count of 16384, and it is sixteenth beats and not whole beats that are counted (giving a maximum sequence length of 1024 whole beats). When a song pointer message is sent, the transmitting equipment sends out the value currently in its counter, and the receiving sequencer then automatically sets its counter to this figure.

This assumes that both pieces of equipment support the song pointer facility, which is by no means a foregone conclusion in reality. This is perhaps a pity, since it is an extremely useful feature. Without it there may be no way of starting two sequencers mid-song at precisely the same point. Note that there is a possible flaw in this system in that it can take a sequencer a significant time to reset itself to the new position in the song. This could cause problems with the sequence being restarted prematurely. The MIDI specification does not set down a minimum time that should be allowed between a song pointer message being sent and a sequence being commenced.

The song pointer message consists of three bytes, which are the status byte plus two data bytes. The seven usable bits of each byte are combined to give a 14 bit number (with the least significant byte being sent first). Fourteen bits gives a range (when converted to decimal numbers) of 0 to 16383, and it is this that limits the system to a maximum of 16384 sixteenth beats.

Tune request

'Tune' in this case does not mean tune in the melody sense, but tune as in to tune an instrument. Some instruments have an automatic tuning facility, and when this is invoked the instrument's pitch is accurately adjusted so that it precisely matches a reference oscillator. This usually means tuning middle A to the standard concert pitch of 440 Hz. A tune request message can be issued from a MIDI controller to automatically tune all the instruments in the system, or those that have this feature implemented anyway.

This message is simply an instruction to switch on a built-in function of those instruments in the system that include it. Each instrument is tuned against its own internal reference, and not against a timing signal provided via the MIDI link. It is therefore a single byte instruction which has no data bytes. Although all the instruments are not tuned to a common reference signal, the individual references should be accurate enough to ensure that there is no noticeable difference in the pitch of the instruments.

System real-time

The system real-time messages are the ones concerned with synchronization of drum machines, or other sequencers which use timing pulses for synchronization purposes. Apart from the timing pulses themselves, there are start, stop, continue, reset, and active sensing messages. These are forms of system message, and accordingly they do not carry channel number information. An interesting point about the instructions is that they take precedence over all other messages, and can be sent at any time. This apparently means that they can be sent in the middle of another instruction, such as a 'note on' or 'note off' type! MIDI can only handle complete bytes of information, and system real-time messages can be sent between the bytes of a multi-byte message. These messages can not be sent mid-byte. It is for this reason that all status bytes have their most significant bit set to 1, and all data bytes have this bit set to 0. A system real-time message can then always be distinguished from data, even if it is mixed in with the data of another message. All system real-time instructions (like the tune request message) are single byte types.

Stop-go

The start and stop instructions are self explanatory. The continue instruction differs from the start type in that it causes the sequence to continue from where it was halted by a stop message, whereas a start instruction causes the sequence to start at the beginning. If a song pointer position message is used to direct the sequencers to the middle of a song, a continue instruction should be used to start the sequence from this position. The start message will always start a sequence from the very beginning.

The system reset message does more than reset any sequencing equipment in the system, it resets every item of equipment in the setup. In other words, it takes each piece of equipment back to the state it was in at power up, and is equivalent to switching everything off and then on again. This could be useful with instruments where you can program them to have a particular start-up state. The start-up parameters would be set to the ones that would normally be required, and a system reset message then provides an easy way of getting back to these parameters, perhaps in the event of some controls being accidentally moved from the required settings. This could be very helpful for live performances. Not all instruments implement this feature, and it is unlikely to be found on disk based instruments such as sound samplers. These can not produce any sounds until data has been loaded from disk, and resetting such an instrument to its (soundless) start-up condition would be pointless.

Clock messages

The clock messages are the equivalent to the clock pulses used for synchronizing conventional drum machines. Although you may encounter references to the MIDI clock, these are not simple clock pulses of the conventional variety, but are single byte MIDI messages sent continuously at regular intervals by the MIDI controller. These timing messages are sent at the rate of 24 per crotchet (quarter note). They keep the drum machines in the system properly synchronized with the start, stop and continue messages being used to get the instruments to start and stop in unison. This is a departure from the conventional method of synchronization where the instruments are started and stopped by switching the clock signal on and off. As already pointed out, the MIDI clock signal is sent all the time, regardless of whether or not a sequence is actually in progress. The original MIDI clock signals were organized in a different way incidentally, but few instruments which used this earlier method were ever produced. There are certainly no new instruments on sale which use the earlier (and now totally obsolete) system.

MIDI timing messages are irrelevant to many instruments and other pieces of equipment which can not generate them and do not have any facilities that could meaningfully receive them. Built-in sequencers are now quite common on keyboard instruments though, and these often have the ability to utilize MIDI timing information. Not all built-in sequencers can both generate and synchronize to MIDI timing messages, and this point is something which needs to be checked carefully by referring to the manuals for your instruments.

Active sensing

This is an optional message which is not implemented in many pieces of equipment. The basic idea is for the MIDI controller to send out this message periodically during periods when there are no other instructions being sent to its output. The MIDI specification states that this message should be sent at intervals of 300 ms (i.e. 0.3 seconds) or less. Any instrument that receives these messages should function normally, if the MIDI system is connected up properly and is functioning correctly. If the active sensing signals should cease to be received, then the instrument should switch off all its voices. This avoids having an instrument stuck with some of its voices producing notes, perhaps because someone has tripped over a cable and broken it, so that the note off messages were never received.

Although this is a desirable feature, it has probably not been considered sufficiently worthwhile to have been widely implemented. It may at first appear to have the disadvantage of increasing MIDI activity, and possibly causing overloads at times of very high activity. This is not the case though, as the active sensing messages only need to be sent if there is no other MIDI activity, and they are not a continuous signal like the system clock messages. By electronic standards they need only be sent very infrequently anyway. Although at one time on the decline, active sensing has been implemented on a number of recent instruments, and could become a standard feature in the future.

Recap

This completes the description of the MIDI codes, and even if you have not followed the fine detail about each one, you should at least have a good idea of the type of messages that can be exchanged via a MIDI connection. In order to start using MIDI effectively all that is really required is the know-how to connect the equipment together, and a basic knowledge of the types of messages that can be handled. If you intend to use any moderately complex setup it is worthwhile putting in the extra effort to gain a more in-depth understanding of the subject. Without such an understanding you may well be able to make quite good use of your system, but you might also be overlooking some very worthwhile features.

MIDI has been designed with a view to the specification evolving and improving as time goes by. This means additions to the specification rather than any major fundamental changes, and the message types described above will hopefully remain in force for many years to come.

Technical manuals

With many pieces of consumer electronics the manuals are largely ignored by the purchasers, who are in many cases not much worse off for having not read them. This is definitely not the case with MIDI equipped instruments. The manual should give the all important details of the particular messages that the equipment recognizes and transmits. There are almost invariably differences between the messages that are recognized and those that the equipment originates. It would be helpful to have a list of the MIDI codes that are not implemented, but you will probably only be able to obtain this information by looking to see what codes are not mentioned. The manuals should also give details of any special features that are available, including system exclusive facilities and any that are the result of new MIDI standards.

MIDI is immensely versatile, but an inevitable consequence of this is that it can take a lot of effort and research in order to set up a system that will provide the features you require. Rushing into things could be a very costly mistake. Looking on the bright side, with the aid of this book you should be able to determine which features you require, and it should then be reasonably easy (if still a little time consuming) to find the equipment that best suits your needs. Having done so, you will have a sophisticated setup that would have cost vast sums of money not so many years ago, and would have probably been in the realms of science fiction 20 to 30 years ago!

Nitty gritty

For most purposes the description of the MIDI language provided so far is all that is needed. If you intend to write MIDI software the situation is different, and you need to know exactly what values are required for each MIDI message. For those who need it, this information is provided below. It is perhaps only fair to point out that the ever popular BASIC programming language is less than ideal for many types of MIDI software. The problem is simply that BASIC is a relatively slow language. If we consider the problems associated with a step-time sequencer, a single channel type could probably be written in BASIC without any problems arising.

Multi-channel operation is a different matter, and to send out note on and note off instructions could easily take more than 100 ms in BASIC. On that basis, to switch on notes on 10 channels would take over a tenth of a second. This would give decidedly ragged timing. Admittedly some modern BASICs could do a little better than this, but many would actually be very much slower. It is unlikely that BASIC could handle real-time sequencing at all, as the bytes of data in multibyte messages are so close together that many bytes would be missed.

For MIDI purposes the speed of assembly language is ideal, or a modern compiled language such as C should give sufficient speed plus the advantages of writing in a high level language. Unlike some digital control systems, MIDI does not place any limit on the maximum duration between bytes in a multi-byte instruction, and in this respect there should be no difficulty in using a slow programming language. However, the speed problems with multi-channel operation and reading MIDI input signals remain a serious limitation for the BASIC programmer.

Channel voice codes

All the channel code messages have the most significant bit of the status byte set to 1, and the least significant nibble carrying the MIDI channel value. Remember that the value used to select a channel is one less than the channel number, because the channels are numbered 1 to 16, but they are selected by values from 0 to 15. With three bits available to specify the type of message, a maximum of eight messages can be accommodated. In fact there are only seven channel message codes, as the eighth code is used for system messages. The table opposite gives details of the binary and decimal values used to select each channel voice message.

In the binary column, cccc represents the bits that carry the channel value. In terms of the decimal number that must be sent to the MIDI port, take the value in the decimal column, add the channel number to it, and deduct one. For example, a note on message on channel 8 would require a value of 151 (144 + 8 = 152, 152 − 1 = 151). Remember that a note on instruction having a velocity value of 0 can be used as a note off instruction.

Binary and decimal values for channel voice messages

Message	Binary	Decimal	No. of data bytes
Note off	1000cccc	128	2
Note on	1001cccc	144	2
Poly key pressure	1010cccc	160	2
Control change	1011cccc	176	2
Program change	1100cccc	192	1
Overall key pressure	1101cccc	208	1
Pitch wheel	1110cccc	224	2

The next table gives the functions of the data bytes for the channel voice messages. All data bytes are in the range 0 to 127.

Channel voice message data bytes

Message	Byte 1	Byte 2
Note off	Note value	Velocity value
Note on	Note value	Velocity value
Poly key pressure	Note value	Pressure value
Control change	Control number	New control value
Program change	Program number	
Overall key pressure	Pressure value	
Pitch wheel	Least significant byte	Most significant byte

With the pitch wheel message the two data bytes are combined to give a single 14 bit number. The true value sent is therefore obtained by multiplying the first byte by 128 and then adding it to the second data byte. For instance, data bytes of 28 and 79 provide a pitch wheel value of 3663 ($28 \times 128 = 3584$, $3584 + 79 = 3663$). A value of 8192 (data bytes of 64 and 0) provides zero pitch change. As explained previously, the same system can be used with the variable controls, by pairing them so as to give two data bytes. For controls that only give an on/off action (i.e. controls 64 to 95) only values of 0 (off) and 127 (on) are valid, and other values will be ignored. Note that the controls are numbered from 0 to 127, and not 1 to 128. Therefore, unlike selecting a channel, the value actually used is the same as the control number.

Channel mode messages

Channel mode messages use the same header code as the control change message, and are accessed with a first data byte having a value between 122 and 127. Details of the channel mode messages are provided in the next table.

Channel mode message data bytes

Control no.	Function	Data byte
121	Reset all controls	Always 0
122	Local control	0 = off, 127 = on
123	All notes off	Always 0
124	Omni mode off	Always 0
125	Omni mode on	Always 0
126	Mono mode on	Number of channels, or 0 to use all channels
127	Poly mode on	Always 0

Obviously, when the mono mode is switched on, the poly mode is switched off, and vice versa. A mode change switches off all notes, but switching local control on or off does not. This feature, and the separate all notes off instruction, should be considered as a safety net feature to prevent notes being accidentally left switched on, and not an alternative to the normal note off message. In fact it does not seem to be a requirement that MIDI equipment actually responds to any form of all notes off instruction, and this part of the MIDI specification is, to say the least, less than entirely clear. The next table shows the controllers that must be written to in order to obtain each of the four standard MIDI modes.

In order to be certain of selecting any MIDI mode, the appropriate two controllers must be activated. Remember that the mono on message must include (in the second data byte) the number of channels to be used in the mono mode, or a value of 0 if all channels are to be used in this mode.

Controller numbers for the four MIDI modes

Mode 1 (omni on/poly)	125 and 127
Mode 2 (omni on/mono)	125 and 126
Mode 3 (omni off/poly)	124 and 127
Mode 4 (omni off/mono)	124 and 126

System messages

The system real-time messages all consist of a single byte with the most significant nibble set at 1111 (240 in decimal). Some other system messages do include a data byte or bytes, but they also have all bits in the most significant nibble set to 1. The least significant nibble is not required for channel identification purposes, and these four bits are used to identify the instruction. This gives a maximum of 16 different system messages. The binary and decimal values needed for the system real-time messages are listed below:

Binary and decimal values for system real-time messages

Binary	Decimal	Message type
11111000	248	Clock signal
11111001	249	Undefined
11111010	250	Start
11111011	251	Continue
11111100	252	Stop
11111101	253	Undefined
11111110	254	Active sensing
11111111	255	System reset

These system real-time messages can be sent at any time, even in the middle of other messages. The system reset instruction must not be sent at switch-on, or when equipment is reset. This could easily result in the system hanging up with reset messages being circulated indefinitely! The clock signals are sent at a rate of 24 per quarter note. Active sensing is optional (and very little used in current MIDI equipment).

Because it is optional, receiving equipment will not automatically switch off all notes in its absence. Equipment that does implement this feature will only switch off all notes after at least one active sensing byte has been received, and there has then been a gap of more than 300 ms since the last message of this type was received.

System exclusive

The system exclusive message starts with the binary code 11110000 (240 decimal) and finishes with the binary code 11110111 (247 decimal). There is no limit to the number of bytes that can be inserted between the system exclusive start and finish messages, but they must all have the most significant bit set to 0. This is to ensure that the data bytes are not mistaken as status bytes (remember that system real-time messages can be inserted into other MIDI messages, including system exclusive types). Any status byte other than a system real-time type will cause a system exclusive message to be terminated. The second byte in a system exclusive message is the manufacturer's identification code, and this table gives a list of manufacturers and their respective codes (in binary and decimal).

Manufacturer identification codes

Manufacturer	Binary	Decimal
SCI	00000001	1
Big Briar	00000010	2
Octave/Plateau	00000011	3
Moog	00000100	4
Passport Designs	00000101	5
Lexicon	00000110	6
Ensoniq	00001111	15
Oberheim	00010000	16
Bon Tempi	00100000	32
SIEL	00100001	33
Kawai	01000000	64
Roland	01000001	65
Korg	01000010	66
Yamaha	01000011	67
Casio	01000100	68

System common

The next list is for the system common messages. The song select status byte is followed by a single data byte which is the song number, and is from 0 to 127. This selects the sequence that will be played when a system real-time start message is received by the sequencer. The song pointer status byte is followed by two data bytes which are combined to give a 14 bit number (with the least significant byte being sent first). This can be used to set the sequencer to a certain point in the selected sequence. Some codes in this category are, as yet, undefined. The system exclusive instructions have been included in this list so that they are available for quick reference purposes, but they are not strictly speaking system common messages.

System common messages and codes

Message	Binary	Decimal	Data bytes
Start system excl.	11110000	240	Maker's code/etc.
Undefined	11110001	241	—
Song position	11110010	242	LS byte/MS byte
Song select	11110011	243	Song no.
Undefined	11110100	244	—
Undefined	11110101	245	—
Tune request	11110110	246	None
End system excl.	11110111	247	None

Sample dump

There have been moves towards standardizing further MIDI features, and in particular, towards standardizing the transfer of sound sample data. This type of transfer can be accomplished under system exclusive messages, with each manufacturer devising their own system, but it would obviously be preferable to have a general system, particularly for those who are using sound samplers from more than one manufacturer. Such a standard does exist, but it is only fair to point out that not all manufacturers actually use it.

Brief technical details of the sample dump standard (SDS) are provided here for those who wish to delve into this aspect of MIDI. It operates using system exclusive messages, with 01111110 (126 in decimal) as the 'manufacturer's' code number. This type of message has been given the paradoxical name of 'universal system exclusive'. Data is sent in groups of bytes known as packets which can each be up to 127 bytes long. What differentiates a packet system from one that simply uses bursts of data is that in a packet system each burst of data includes an identification number. In a basic system the sending equipment sends a packet, waits momentarily for it to be processed, sends another one, and so on until all the data has been sent. The system also allows for a more complicated setup in which the MIDI IN and OUT sockets of the two pieces of equipment are cross coupled. This allows the flow of data to be controlled, with the receiving equipment sending a 'wait' instruction in order to prevent a further packet being sent for the time being, or an 'acknowledge' message when it is ready to receive more data. A simple form of what in computing is generally termed 'handshaking'. This system also permits error checking and correction to be implemented via a simple set of rules known as protocols.

Channels

The system is quite sophisticated, and it includes a system of channelling that enables up to 127 pieces of equipment to be individually accessed (although most instruments will probably just use the standard 0–15 MIDI channels here, since more than 16 instruments are unlikely to be used in practice). There is also provision for addressing of sound samples so that a particular sample can be requested. The address is actually a two byte type, but it is difficult to envisage a system that would fully exploit this feature, even one based on a mass storage device such as a hard disk. On the other hand, if data storage technology moves on sufficiently, this system will be very well placed to exploit it.

The SDS system is based on seven types of message, as detailed below. All these messages start with the system exclusive status byte followed by the universal manufacturers' code. These are therefore omitted in the message descriptions that follow. All finish with the 'system exclusive end' message, which in consequence has also been omitted from the message descriptions. Note that this includes each group of data bytes, which are sent as a series of separate messages. This is virtually essential if the handshaking and error checking systems are to be implemented effectively. The fourth byte is the code for each of the seven instructions. In these descriptions these code numbers are given in binary, but the decimal values are also provided (the numbers in brackets).

Dump request
Channel number, 00000011 (3) sample number (LSB), sample number (MSB).

Acknowledge
Channel number, 01111111 (127), packet number.

Not acknowledged (i.e. error detected)
Channel number, 01111110 (126), packet number.

Cancel (i.e. abort the data transfer)
Channel number, 01111101 (125), packet number.

Wait
Channel number, 01111100 (124), packet number.

Header
Channel number, 00000001 (1).
Sample number (LS byte), sample number (MS byte).
Sample format.
Sample period (LS byte), sample period (middle byte), sample period (MS byte).
Sample length (LS byte), sample length (middle byte), sample length (MS byte).
Loop start (LS byte), loop start (middle byte), loop start (MS byte).
Loop end (LS byte), loop end (middle byte), loop end (MS byte).
Loop type.

Data packet
Channel number, 00000010 (2), running packet count, data (120 bytes), checksum.

The header contains some important information including a three byte number which gives the sampling frequency. In fact the figure here is not strictly speaking the sampling frequency, but the period of each sample in nanoseconds (a nanosecond is one thousand millionth of a second). Dividing one million by the figure used here therefore gives the sampling frequency in kilohertz. This method permits a very wide range of frequencies to be covered and provides excellent resolution. The sample length is in words (i.e. complete samples) and not bytes. The sample format indicates the number of bits per sample, and the valid range is from 8 to 28. Only linear sampling is supported, and software conversion must be used with logarithmic samples. The loop

63

type value is 0 for forwards only, or 1 for forwards/backwards operation. Other loop types will probably be defined in the future, and the system supports a maximum of 128 different types. The checksum in the data packets uses a system of XORing.

Once again, I must stress the importance of studying equipment manuals in order to determine which MIDI codes are actually implemented, and to determine what system exclusive messages (if any) are available. Remember, the list of recognized messages for most pieces of equipment is different to the types of message that can be transmitted.

4 MIDI computing

Although microcomputers may not seem to have a great deal to do with most electronic instruments, there must be very few instruments produced these days that are not based on one. We are not just talking about the up-market synthesizers and sound samplers either – even quite inexpensive instruments are computer based these days. Some of the more sophisticated instruments actually contain more than one microprocessor, and a computer controlled system with a number of instruments could well contain more than a dozen microprocessors in total. There is no absolute necessity to use microprocessors in electronic instruments, and other hardware could perform the necessary functions, but the advantage of using a microprocessor is the great versatility it provides. This versatility is demonstrated by the fact that from time to time manufacturers have been known to bring out upgraded versions of an instrument where the hardware is in fact no different from the original. The extra features have been provided by changing the software that controls the unit. This ease with which new ideas can be implemented has done much to speed up the development of electronic musical instruments. It has also helped to make highly sophisticated instruments more affordable.

What a microprocessor does

An in-depth study of microprocessors would be out of place here, but even a very basic understanding of the principles involved is of major advantage to anyone dealing with modern electronic musical instruments. If you look at a few sophisticated MIDI systems, the chances are that most of them will be built around a home or personal computer. In order to exploit MIDI fully, a computer based system is required, and budding MIDI experts would be well advised to gain as much computer expertise as they can. Here we will consider some of the more important aspects of microprocessors and computers, but we will only consider things on a fairly superficial level. This gives a useful overview that should help to dispel a few myths. It will not give the sort of detailed information you will need in order to use computer systems, but equipment and software manuals should provide specific instructions for any computer equipment and software you obtain. It should also help to give a better idea of what sort of equipment you will need, and the types of MIDI software you can run on it.

In points of detail computer systems vary enormously, but they all use a fundamental setup of the type outlined in Fig. 4.1. The display could be anything from a few LEDs to a high resolution colour monitor giving a complex graphics output. Similarly, the keyboard could be just a few switches, or a large typewriter style keyboard with over a hundred keys. Either way, these represent the main means for the user to input data to the computer, and the computer to provide information to the user. In fact with many modern computers and music software a 'mouse' is the main method of controlling the system, and we will look at these a little later. The input/output ports enable the computer to communicate with peripheral equipment such as printers and disk drives, but in a MIDI context the most important input and output ports are the MIDI IN and MIDI OUT sockets.

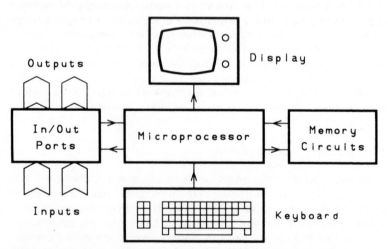

Figure 4.1 A basic computer system consists of a keyboard, microprocessor, memory, input/output ports and a display

Memory

The memory is used to store information. This information can be program instructions, or data for the program to work on. People are often sceptical when they are told that all a computer does is to shuffle numbers around, doing operations like taking a number from an input port and storing it in memory. This is perfectly true, but put in this insipid way it is a bit misleading, and can make microprocessors look rather useless. They are clearly far from useless, and perform countless valuable functions. The salient point is that the numbers that are being shuffled around are meaningful pieces of data when taken in context.

As an example, the microprocessor could be taking in numbers from an input port and storing them in memory. The system could incorporate a timer circuit (or this could be implemented by a software routine) so that together with each input value stored in memory, the time between that value and the previous one could also be stored. Another program could be used to take each input value stored in memory, and send it to an output port. Again, a timer implemented in hardware or software could be used, and it would use the timing information stored in memory to regulate the flow of data to the output port. In this way data being sent from the output port would be made an accurate reconstruction of the data originally received at the input port.

This still may not seem particularly useful, but suppose that the numbers received from the input port were MIDI note values, and that they were outputted to a MIDI output. This gives the basis of a MIDI real-time sequencer. Actually things are a bit more complicated than could be handled by this simple routine, as the incoming MIDI information would be groups of three bytes. However, the programs could easily be designed to read groups of three bytes into memory, together with the timing information. The program could also be made to check that the incoming data was note on and note off information, or other relevant MIDI data, and to discard any irrelevant data such as MIDI clock signals.

Conditional instructions

Microprocessors have conditional instructions that make this sort of thing possible. The program would take in a byte of data, and it would then check this value to see if it matched a reference value held in memory, and if it did, a certain course of action would then be taken. Current microprocessors cannot operate on the basis of reading a value, and performing one of several possible actions depending on what the value happens to be. They can perform this sort of task, but only by going through a whole series of comparisons until a match is obtained. An alternative method is to use the input value as a pointer to a memory address, with the data at that address then directing the program to the place in memory where it will find the start of the appropriate routine to perform.

Continuing with our real-time sequencer theme, microprocessor based systems can usually implement extra features just by improving the software. As an example, a common facility on real-time sequencers is the ability to vary the playback speed via some form of tempo control. Using the mathematical capabilities of a microprocessor this type of function is easily implemented. It is simply a matter of multiplying the stored timer values by a certain amount in order to slow down the playback process, or dividing the timer values by a certain amount in order to speed up the process. It is not necessary for the microprocessor to go through the timer values stored in memory and change them all. The multiplication or division can be performed on each timer value when it is read during playback.

Most single computer instructions are very basic and do not achieve very much, but by using large numbers of them it is possible for complex tasks to be performed. Microprocessors are relatively slow by general electronic standards, but they can still perform large numbers of instructions per second. Some can perform more than a million program instructions per second, and although each instruction is a fairly simple action, this is nevertheless sufficient to permit quite complex programs to be performed at adequate speed. Well written software running on any reasonably powerful system should certainly be able to implement a 'bells and whistles' feature without grinding to a halt under the load.

System management

Proper management of the memory circuits is clearly crucial to the correct operation of a microprocessor system. Memory must be organized in a way that enables any desired piece of data or any required program instruction to be located. This is achieved using a setup of the type shown in Fig. 4.2. The data bus is the collection of interconnections which carry the data from one part of the system to another. In the past this has been an 8 bit bus for most computers, but 16 bit types are now quite commonplace in both business and home computing. There are now even some readily available 32 bit types. As MIDI applications are largely involved with the processing of 8 bit bytes of data, the use of a 16 or 32 bit data bus does not in itself offer any great advantage. There are advantages to 16 and 32 bit computers for MIDI applications though, and one of these is that they generally

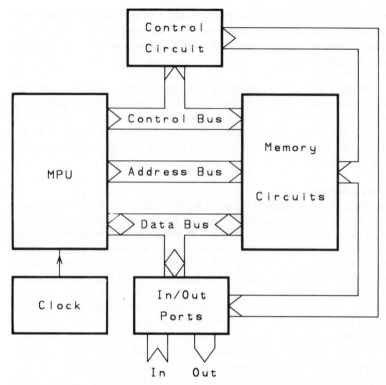

Figure 4.2 Within the computer, control signals, address information and data are all moved around on 'buses'

operate somewhat faster than 8 bit machines, even when performing relatively simple tasks. Perhaps the main advantage in the present context is that they can handle vast amounts of memory efficiently, whereas 8 bit machines tend to offer comparatively small amounts of memory that are often less than fully utilized.

The microprocessor selects the desired memory circuit by placing the appropriate number on the address bus. The address bus is invariably more bits wide than the data bus, and for 8 bit microprocessors a 16 bit address bus is more or less standard. This gives an address range of 0 to 65535, or some 65536 different addresses. This would normally be referred to as 64 k rather than 65536 bytes. One k of memory is enough to store 1024 bytes, and although 1024 may seem an odd amount to select, it is perhaps more logical than using 1000.

Bear in mind that microprocessors work in binary numbers, and that the range of numbers available with a 10 bit bus is 0 to 1023 (i.e. 1024 different values). Incidentally, the type of memory used for storing data and programs is random access memory, or RAM as it is more usually termed.

Although 64 k was at one time considered to be a massive amount of data storage, computing has moved on, and computer programs have become more complex. MIDI in particular, is an application that can require large amounts of data to be held in memory, and often involves the use of complex graphics (which eat up large chunks of memory space).

8 bit limitations

This 64 k limit has proved to be extremely restrictive and renders standard 8 bit machines unable to handle the more demanding applications really well. Computer manufacturers have tried to overcome this by devising ways of installing larger amounts of memory in their 8 bit machines. This is not very difficult technically, and it is usually achieved by bank switching. This simply means having two or more 64 k blocks of memory, and an output port which is used to select one of them. In this way it is possible to have almost limitless memory installed in a computer, but it is an inefficient system. The microprocessor's instructions are designed with the 64 k maximum in mind, and they do not automatically adjust to suit any form of extended memory. It is up to the programmer to find a way of handling the extra memory properly, and this can often be awkward in practice.

More specifically, applications that require a lot of switching between memory banks tend to be slow, and with even the slightest deficiency in the program the system will crash. There have been a number of 8 bit microcomputers available with 128 k or more of memory, but surprisingly little software that takes advantage of it. I have had two 128 k 8 bit machines, but only a couple of programs which actually recognized the existence of the extra bank of memory. One of these was a word processor which used the simple expedient of having the program in one bank, and the data in the other. As the program and display generator only used about half the first bank of memory, even this arrangement only exploited about 75% of the available memory.

Most 16 and 32 bit computers have wide address buses, or are designed to use some form of bank switching, and can handle large amounts of memory properly. By large amounts I mean about 512 k to one megabyte or more fitted as standard, with the option of fitting several more megabytes of RAM if required. A megabyte is equal to

1024 k incidentally. This is sufficient for virtually all applications, including sophisticated MIDI software.

Reading and writing

The control bus is used to ensure that everything in the system is set to the correct operating mode. The address bus is a set of outputs on the microprocessor, but the data bus is bidirectional. The same set of connections are used to transfer data into memory, and to read it back again. The control bus, usually with the aid of some simple circuitry, is used by the microprocessor to switch the memory circuit to the 'read' or 'write' mode, as required. This ensures that the disastrous situation where both the microprocessor and the memory circuits are trying to place data on to the data bus simultaneously is avoided.

The input/output ports must also be controlled in the same way, as they utilize the bidirectional data bus. In fact these ports would in virtually all cases be fed with the address bus via some simple decoding circuits. With some microprocessors there is no distinction between memory and input/output ports at all. Data is fed to them and read back from them in precisely the same way. It is up to the programmer to ensure that the two are never confused. With other microprocessors a line or lines of the control bus are used to switch between the memory and input/output circuits, and they are accessed via separate sets of instructions.

Clock circuit

A clock circuit provides a regular train of pulses that are used to move the microprocessor from one part of an instruction to the next. Apart from a few recent exceptions, it is not correct to assume that one instruction is carried out per clock pulse. The number of clock pulses per instruction depends on the complexity of each instruction, and on the design of the microprocessor. What this means in practice is that you cannot assume that one computer is faster in operation than another simply because it has a higher clock rate. Even where two computers are based on microprocessors of the same type, the fact that one has a higher clock frequency than the other does not necessarily mean that it is faster. Some computers are a bit sluggish as they have slow memory circuits, and they have to be put in 'wait' states, which is when the microprocessor is literally waiting for the memory circuits to catch up before it moves on to the next operation.

Another failing of some computers is that they rely on the microprocessor to provide virtually every feature of the computer unaided, whereas other computers back up the microprocessor with complex video generator circuits, timer circuits, etc., that leave the micro-

71

processor largely free to get on with other tasks. A further point to bear in mind, is that how well or otherwise the software is written has at least as much effect on running speed as does the performance of the computer. Well written software will not transform a mediocre computer into a top notch one, but poorly written software can effectively turn a powerful 16 bit computer into a sub-standard 8 bit one. The only way to judge the effectiveness of a computer and software package is to try them out, preferably over a period of time. Unfortunately, a quick demonstration in a shop is the most you are likely to obtain.

The display and keyboard are not shown in Fig. 4.2, but these are really part of the input/output section of a computer. They keyboard is usually read via a simple input port, but most computers have complex display driver circuits which enable text and graphics displays to be easily generated. A computer which has reasonably good graphics capability is a decided asset for MIDI use.

Incidentally, in Fig. 4.2 the microprocessor is labelled MPU, and this stands for microprocessor unit. You may encounter the alternative term of CPU, or central processing unit.

Versatility

If we return to our earlier example of using a computer system to act as a real-time sequencer, the same basic setup will also operate as a sound sampler! Instead of a MIDI input and a MIDI output, the system would need analogue to digital and digital to analogue converters. These respectively convert an input voltage to a proportional digital value, and convert a digital value to a proportional output voltage. By taking samples of the audio input at a high enough rate, storing them in memory, and then outputting them as required, the original audio signal (or something close to it anyway) can be produced as and when needed. The pitch of the sound can be raised or lowered by outputting the values either more rapidly or more slowly than the original samples were taken. In this way sound samplers can record one note, but produce an output at any desired pitch over a range of several octaves.

Whereas in a real-time sequencer application the average rate at which values would be stored would probably be a few dozen per second, for sound sampling it would normally be a few thousand or even tens of thousands per second. This higher rate is still within the capabilities of a microprocessor though, and most sound samplers are microprocessor based. Multi-timbral sound sampling is perhaps beyond most microprocessors, and this is normally achieved using what are virtually separate sampler circuits with a common control circuit.

Microprocessors have many other uses in electronic musical instruments, and are even used in some analogue synthesizers. In a traditional synthesizer circuit the keyboard is a simple switch and resistor arrangement that gives a series of output voltages that are used to control the VCO. This arrangement was dropped in many of the later analogue synthesizers in favour of a system which has a microprocessor monitoring the keyboard, and producing the appropriate output voltage by way of a digital to analogue converter. This may seem like an unnecessarily convoluted way of tackling the problem, but it does have advantages. A problem with the older type of keyboard is that pressing more than one key at a time can produce a note that is nonexistent on the normal musical scale. Most instruments of this type have additional keyboard switches and circuitry that avoids this, and produces the note that corresponds to the lowest or highest key to be pressed.

Digital keyboard

This problem is avoided completely with the digital scanning method, as the keyboard reading system is arranged so that the microprocessor can tell exactly which key or keys have been pressed, even if a number of keys are operated at once. The software determines which note will sound if more than one key at a time is pressed. Instruments which use this system often give the choice of having the highest, lowest, or last note that was pressed. This system lends itself well to polyphonic instruments, where a single set of keyboard switches is all that is needed. The microprocessor can ascertain which key or keys have been pressed, and then send the appropriate voltages to the instrument's voice generator circuits via digital to analogue converters. Using an analogue keyboard circuit polyphonic operation is very difficult to implement properly.

When microprocessors were invented they were not a new idea in search of problems to solve. There were a multitude of applications just waiting for the microprocessor to make them practical, and many of these are in the sphere of electronic music. Microprocessors are to be found in many electronic musical instruments because they do the job much better and cheaper than the alternatives, and they are the natural choice. A personal computer, via MIDI, fits perfectly into an electronic music setup. Computers and most electronic music instruments both talk the same digital language, and MIDI provides the physical link and the protocol for them to exchange messages.

Which computer?

Newcomers to computing tend to look at computer hardware first, and having selected a likely looking setup, buy it and then look for suitable software to run on it. This is definitely doing things the wrong way round, as I have found to my cost in the past! It is much more sensible to look for computer programs that provide the functions you require, and then buy the hardware that is needed to run the software properly. With this method the computer equipment largely chooses itself, and there are unlikely to be any difficult decisions to make. Of course, when doing things this way you have to keep in mind the overall cost of the system, and choose something within your budget.

I suppose that many people already own personal computers, and in this case it only makes sense to look for suitable software for your existing machine before contemplating buying a new computer for MIDI purposes. This search may prove to be fruitless as MIDI software is not available for every computer. Also, few computers have a built-in MIDI port, and you will probably need an add-on MIDI interface as well as compatible software. If the MIDI interface and the software are not purchased as a single package, do make quite sure that the software is compatible with the interface. Most add-on MIDI interfaces fit on to the computer's 'expansion port', or some similar port. It then connects straight on to the computer's buses, and is slotted into a previously unused area of the input/output address map. If the software is not designed for use with the MIDI interface you have fitted, it may send out data to the wrong address and read it back from the wrong address. There are some standards that have been agreed by MIDI interface manufacturers, formally or otherwise, but it still makes sense not to take any chances, and to check compatibility before parting with any money.

As pointed out in a previous chapter, the MIDI method of asynchronous serial data transfer is very similar to the standard RS232C system (and the similar RS423 type as used on some Acorn computers and a few others). For computers that have a port of this type, an obvious form of add-on MIDI interface would be an RS232C/RS423 to MIDI adaptor. This method does not seem to have been adopted to any great extent in practice. Only some very basic signal processing is required in order to permit standard serial interfaces to drive MIDI inputs, and to enable MIDI outputs to drive standard serial inputs. This therefore offers a very inexpensive means of adding MIDI capability to suitable computers. Possibly this system has not been widely accepted due to an inability of many serial interfaces to operate at the MIDI baud rate, which is not a standard RS232C/RS423 rate. Anyway, it is the standard system of MIDI interfacing for the Commodore Amiga computer, and all MIDI software for this particular machine seems to assume that MIDI communications will be established via the serial port.

With a lot of add-on MIDI interfaces you will find that there is more than just single MIDI IN and OUT sockets. There will often be a THRU socket plus one or two extra outputs as well. Presumably the computer will be used as the MIDI controller, and there is then no obvious use for the MIDI THRU socket, although there is no harm in having it there just in case it should be needed at some time. The output sockets (on all the add-on MIDI units I have encountered anyway), all provide the same signal, and are not independent MIDI outputs. This is a very useful feature as a surprisingly large number of MIDI instruments do not include a THRU socket. Extra MIDI outputs enable the star method of connection to be adopted without having to obtain a MIDI THRU-Box.

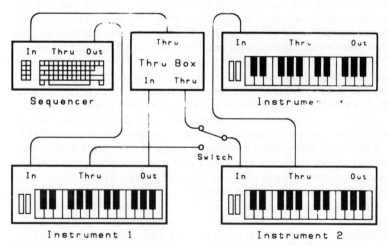

Figure 4.3 A system of switching between keyboard and sequencer control

Software support

Commodore 64 and C128

Some computers are supported by large amounts of MIDI software and general electronic music gadgetry, while for others there is comparatively little available. Probably the best supported 8 bit machine is the Commodore 64, and its derivatives such as the C128. This is not because it is particularly well suited to MIDI use, but because it was popular with musicians early on due to its better than average built-in sound generator circuit. These users naturally wanted to progress to MIDI control when MIDI started to feature on new instruments, and some excellent software and hardware has been produced to meet this demand. The Acorn BBC model B series of computers are also quite well supported by music software and add-ons, and this machine should not be overlooked in the 8 bit stakes. Probably the cheapest way to set up a good computer system for MIDI use is to obtain a good second-hand Commodore 64 or BBC Model B system.

Atari ST

The extra computing power and memory of 16 bit computers is something that can be put to good use in many MIDI applications. The price difference between 16 bit and 8 bit machines was once vast, but the gap has been steadily narrowing and has now been virtually squeezed out of existence. In particular, the computers at the bottom end of the Atari ST range are not much more expensive than the better 8 bit machines, and are in fact cheaper than some. The Atari ST computers are the nearest thing to a 'standard' MIDI computer, and not just because they are equipped with built-in MIDI input and output ports. This has undoubtedly helped to establish the ST computers in this field, but they also have a powerful microprocessor, plenty of memory, and good graphics capability. This qualifies them to handle any MIDI application well. There is a large range of MIDI software available for these computers, and virtually all of it will run on the cheaper models (one or two programs require 1 megabyte or more of RAM, and will only work with the basic models if they are suitably upgraded). Anyone who is going to build up a computer based MIDI system can certainly not afford to ignore the Atari ST computers and large range of matching MIDI software.

The latest versions of the ST computers are the "STE" machines, which are enhanced STs having superior sound and graphics capabilities. From the MIDI point of view they are not much different to the original STs, and should run all the same programs.

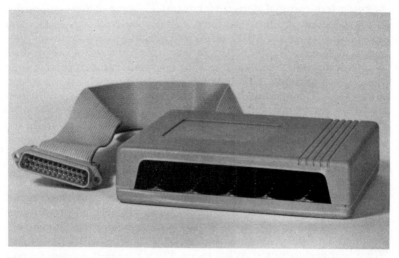

Figure 4.4 The Datel MIDI interface for the Amiga. This provides IN, THRU and three OUT sockets

Commodore Amiga

It would also be a mistake to ignore the other 16 bit machines. The main rivals to the Atari ST computers are the Commodore Amiga range. Like their predecessor, the Commodore 64, these have excellent built-in sound capabilities, but no integral MIDI interface. However, as pointed out previously, an inexpensive interface which fits onto the serial port is all that is needed to provide MIDI compatibility (Fig. 4.4.). They use the same processor as the Atari ST range, and also offer plenty of memory plus excellent graphics. At one time the Amigas lagged well behind the Atari STs in terms of the amount of MIDI software that was available. They still probably lag some way behind in this respect, but there is now quite a range of MIDI software available for the Amiga computers. Unless you wish to use one of the more unusual types of MIDI program, you should be able to find plenty of suitable software for these computers.

Other contenders

The other main contenders in the 16 bit stakes are the IBM machines and the numerous IBM compatible machines. There is a fast growing range of MIDI add-ons and software for these, as well as other music software (educational software for example). Some of these can be difficult to obtain though, and they are not exactly cheap. In fact you should not expect any MIDI software to be in the games software price range. It takes a lot of man-hours (or even man-years) to produce sophisticated MIDI software, and the user base is much smaller than for games programs. This inevitably results in much higher prices, and good MIDI software can easily cost ten times as much as top quality games programs.

32 bit computers and software to match them are a bit thin on the ground at present, but one of the standard add-ons for the powerful Acorn Archimedes RISC machines is a MIDI interface, and this could be the basis of the ultimate MIDI system.

One point about choosing a computer system for MIDI use is that you need to be quite sure that you obtain one that will be powerful enough to satisfy your requirements. Once you start using a computer based MIDI system you are likely to find that before too long you are producing music on a scale and complexity that goes well beyond anything you had expected. What seemed like a powerful system when you bought it could easily seem rather limiting after a few months of use. Upgrading to a more sophisticated system is then likely to be extremely expensive. With any so-called 'power user' application, which certainly includes most MIDI use, there is a lot to be said for purchasing the most sophisticated system you can afford.

WIMPs

A lot of MIDI software is based on a so-called WIMP environment. WIMP is an acronym, and it stands for 'windows-icons-mouse-pointer'. This probably leaves you no wiser, but what it is really about is making computers easier to use, especially for inexperienced users. Computers normally operate in a text mode, and instructions are typed in at the typewriter style keyboard. WIMP software uses the alternative of having a graphics screen (which can include text where necessary) with small pictorial representations of various items. These pictures are the icons, and the desired icon can be selected by moving an on-screen pointer over it and clicking a button on the mouse. The mouse is basically just a small plastic box with some simple circuitry inside that is connected to the computer via a flexible lead (Fig. 4.5). Moving the mouse around on the table top (or in some cases on a special pad) results in corresponding movement of the on-screen pointer. The box is fitted with two or three push button switches which are used to produce certain actions. For example, with most

Figure 4.5 A two button mechanical mouse on its pad

systems simply placing the pointer over an icon will not select that icon. It is usually necessary to click the left hand mouse button, or in some cases, to double-click it (i.e. click it twice in rapid succession).

Window dressing

This leaves only the 'windows' unexplained. The windows are areas of the screen enclosed by a border, and each area can be given over to a different function. With a true WIMP system the windows can be moved around the screen, changed in size, and switched on or off as required.

WIMP systems, or WIMP-like systems are not necessarily any more easy to use then text based systems. They lend themselves better to some applications than to others, and some software designers use this environment better than others. Music applications are perhaps amongst those that are best suited to the WIMP environment, and there is certainly plenty of MIDI software that fully exploits it. As an example of the way this type of system can operate, in a notation program the staves could be placed in the main window. Another window could contain a range of icons with notes and other symbols used in standard music notation. Another window could contain a graphical representation of a piano style keyboard. Moving the pointer on to a note on the keyboard and clicking the mouse could be used to cause that note to be played on the currently selected MIDI channel.

To place notes etc. on the stave it would merely be a matter of using the mouse and pointer to select the icon for the desired symbol, and then to click the mouse with the pointer at the appropriate point on the stave. The note (or whatever) would then be deposited at this point on the stave. Although the pointer is sometimes just a basic arrow style pointer, many pieces of software use something more appropriate. In this example, the pointer could usefully be whatever symbol is currently selected. This is not just gimmickry, and the symbolic pointer would act as a reminder of what particular symbol was currently selected.

The ability to resize and switch off windows might not seem to be a particularly useful one, but it can be more than a little helpful in some circumstances. Staying with our hypothetical notation program, the keyboard icon might be required all the time, but it could well be only of value from time to time. Being able to switch it off and resize the stave window to fill in the vacant area of screen would then be helpful, as it would permit more of the score to be seen on screen at one time.

Pop-down menus

'Pop-down' or 'pull-down' menus are something that go hand in hand with icons and windows (Fig. 4.6). Continuing with our notation

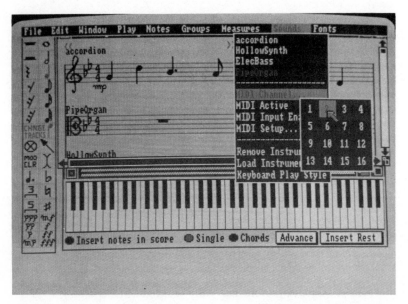

Figure 4.6 A pop-down menu. This one has a sub menu for MIDI channel selection

program example, the icons permit the music to be entered on to the staves, but they do not provide a lot of vital functions that the program must have. This includes functions like selecting the required MIDI channel, getting the program to play the score, copying chunks of the score from one page to another, and so on. These could actually be implemented with the aid of further icons, but if used to excess this system can become confusing rather than easy to use.

Some form of menu system provides a practical solution to the problem. In general, the facilities that will be required a great deal are accessed through icons, while those that will be used infrequently are obtained via a menu. A menu is simply a list of options. Usually there is a series of headings across the top of the screen, and when the pointer is placed on one of these and the appropriate button is pressed, a menu listing a series of options drops down from the heading. For instance, there could be a 'CHANNEL' heading, and when this is selected a menu giving numbers from 1 to 16 could drop down, with the current selection highlighted in some way. The required option is selected by continuing to hold down the mouse button, sliding the pointer down to the required option, and then releasing the button, or using some similar system. The main point of the pop-down menu system is that it normally only occupies a small area at the top of the screen, leaving most of the screen available for the main function of the program.

A well thought out piece of WIMP based software will enable inexperienced computer users to operate the program with relatively little difficulty, and it should in fact enable anyone who is unfamiliar with the program to quickly learn to use it. Some WIMP environment programs I have encountered are so well designed that the manual was virtually superfluous. The only real flaw with WIMP systems is that while they are easy to learn, they are not always very fast to use. Ideally, a WIMP based program that will need the user to enter large amounts of data should give the option of using the mouse or the keyboard to enter data. Experienced users can then learn the key codes needed to control the system, and operate much more quickly.

While a mouse is usually part of the standard equipment supplied with 16 bit computers, and much of the software for these machines takes advantage of a WIMP environment, it is generally considered to be something of a luxury item for 8 bit computers. To handle a true WIMP system really well a fair amount of computing power is needed, and this could leave even the better 8 bit machines struggling slightly. However, a lot of keyboard controlled 8 bit software borrows ideas from WIMP programs.

Disks

A computer's RAM is only suitable for temporary data storage. Apart from the fact that it would soon become full if it was used for storing all your data, the contents of RAM are lost every time the computer is switched off! The standard forms of permanent data storage are ordinary audio compact cassettes, and magnetic disk systems. The latter are like a cross between a magnetic tape recording system and ordinary gramophone records. The disk (which is the shortened version of the full 'diskette' name) is a piece of thin plastic that is coated with a magnetic material and contained in a protective sleeve or casing. Unlike records, a computer disk is not removed from the sleeve before it is used.

In use the disk rotates, and a record/playback head records or reads data that is contained in what is usually 40 or 80 tracks per side. The tracks are concentric, and in this respect computer disks differ from their audio counterparts where a single spiralled track per side is used. Disk systems generally record and play back data at a substantially higher rate than can be achieved using ordinary cassette recorders. This is not their main advantage though. In fact some disk systems (notably the original disk drives for the Commodore 64) operate at a speed which is comparable to the faster cassette systems. They are still far superior because the disk drive can jump almost immediately to any part of any track on a disk. Finding the right piece of data on a cassette tape can be very time consuming, or vast numbers of short cassettes must be used. Disk systems are generally much more reliable than compact cassette data storage systems.

There are several different sizes of disk, and variations of format within each size (single-sided, double-sided, double density, etc.). MIDI applications often require large amounts of data to be stored, and a disk format that provides high storage capacity per disk plus a fast read/write rate is preferable to a low capacity slow format. Any disk system is much better than a cassette system, and is unlikely to greatly increase the overall cost of the system. It is noticeable that instruments which need to store large amounts of data (especially sound samplers) are now mostly supplied with built-in disk drives, and cassette storage systems are now relatively rare on instruments. It is noticeable that most of the more recently introduced computers have integral disk drives and no provision for cassette tape storage.

Hard disks
There is an alternative form of disk drive called a 'hard' disk or 'fixed' disk. It operates in what is essentially the same manner as ordinary

disks, or 'floppy' disks as they are sometimes called. However, a hard disk, as the name implies, has the magnetic coating on a rigid disk. In most cases it is not actually a single disk, but several, mounted one above the other on a common spindle. The 'fixed' disk name is derived from the fact that a disk of this type remains in the drive, and is not interchangeable in the same way as the floppy version. Also, a hard disk rotates continuously at high speed while the computer is switched on.

The point of a hard disk is that it enables data and programs to be stored and read back again at very high rates. The speed at which data can be saved and loaded is likely to be restricted by the rate at which the computer can handle it, rather than by the limitations of the disk itself. With a suitable computer several hundred kilobytes of data can be handled in under a second. Although being unable to change the disk might seem to be a major drawback, hard disks have high storage capacities that are generally about 20 megabytes or more. I am writing this book on a business computer fitted with a 20 megabyte hard disk. Apart from the word processor used to produce the text and the drafting package used for the drawings, the disk also holds a spreadsheet, a printed circuit design program, two programming languages, an accounting package, and a desk-top publishing program, plus data files for these programs. It is still less than two thirds full. Any of these programs can be loaded in a few seconds, as can any data required by one of the programs.

A hard disk is highly desirable, but even though prices have fallen substantially over recent years, they are still quite expensive for most computers. In some cases they still cost more than the computer! For most users (including myself) there are other aspects of the MIDI system where money could more usefully be spent.

A point to keep in mind when selecting software is that some of the more sophisticated programs will only run on a system that is disk based, and in some cases two disk drives might be needed in order to run the program properly. Software writers normally try to design software so that it will run on a fairly basic system, but you should always check that the computer equipment you intend to use will be sufficient to run the programs you choose.

Programs

So far we have considered the basics of how computers operate, what machines are available, and how they are used, but what kinds of MIDI software can be obtained? There seems to be a steady flow of new software and software ideas, which is an encouraging sign. It does mean that here it is only possible to talk in very general terms about the types of software that are available. Magazine advertisements, dealers and literature from software houses will have to be consulted in order to determine exactly what is available. However, the following notes should give you a good idea of what can be achieved, and what type of software is most likely to be of interest to you.

Real-time sequencing

The topic of real-time sequencing is one that has already been covered to some extent in this chapter when dealing with the basics of computer operation. The sequencers which fall into this category differ tremendously in the degree of sophistication they offer. Even a very basic type which simply records MIDI data from a keyboard and then allows it to be played back at the desired tempo is a decided asset for a MIDI system. This feature is often built into MIDI keyboard instruments, and does not really require the sophistication of a home or personal computer. Real-time sequencers, whatever their degree of sophistication, almost invariably include some form of loop facility. This enables a short sequence to be recorded, and then played back over and over again. This is mainly used to provide a repetitive backing for a 'live' performance.

Timing correction

Another feature to be found on many real-time sequencers is a timing correction facility (quantization). The idea of this is to tidy up the timing if it is a little ragged. The computer assumes certain correct time values for the various lengths of notes, and it then compares stored time values with its list of ideal values. It is then just a matter of changing each of the stored values to the nearest ideal one. Ideally this feature should operate only during playback so that you have the option of using, or not. Some sequencers provide the timing correction only while recording. This may be put forward by the advertising men as a great asset, but it is usually the result of the timing information only being stored in memory with very low resolution, so as to minimize the amount of memory used. This type of quantization could reasonably be considered as a failing rather than a desirable asset. Some quantization systems do not work particularly well, and can result in problems like brief notes being edited out. This type of thing is avoidable, and most modern sequencers have good quantization systems.

Edit a note

Perhaps the most useful feature a real-time sequencer can have is some form of manual editing facility. A timing correction process of the type described above gives perfect results provided the original playing was not too bad, but it can also give rather 'mechanical' sounding results. A manual system of correction enables any serious errors to be corrected without rendering the rest of the piece expressionless.

This is where the graphics of a proper computer display such as a medium or high resolution monitor can be put to good use. Rather than the note durations simply being presented as a list of figures, they can be represented graphically on the screen, perhaps as lines having lengths that are proportional to the note durations. Changing the length of a line, perhaps using a mouse and on-screen pointer, would then alter the length of the note it represents. This sort of graphical representation can make it much easier to go through a piece and make the desired alterations, particularly with multichannel sequencing. This is an area in which a real-time sequencer based on a personal computer really scores over one that is built into an instrument. Even a mediocre computer display can show vast amounts of data on a single screen, and this makes editing far quicker and easier. Apart from a few exceptions, most instruments have only a very basic built-in display and no facility to add an external monitor. Any editing facilities are often comparatively crude, and may be practically unusable in practice.

It is not only the note durations that can be edited; the note values can also be adjusted if necessary. If a sequence is played perfectly apart from one or two wrong notes, rather than redoing the whole piece, the appropriate values stored in memory can be manually altered. Not every piece of real-time sequencer software offers this type of editing feature, but it is a very powerful one which is well worth having. Again, the excellent display capabilities of a personal computer can make this type of editing very much more straightforward than using something like a simple two digit LED display. In fact this type of editing is only likely to be available on systems where a fairly sophisticated display is available.

Multi-tracking

Most real-time sequencers permit tracks to be recorded one at a time so that a complex piece of music can be built up. This is analogous to multi-track tape recording, and some sequencer software provides tape recorder style controls (play, fast-forward, stop, etc.) to help make the system more user-friendly. Apart from being able to edit pieces in a way that is impossible with traditional multi-track recording, the MIDI recording studio approach has the advantage that there is no build-up of tape noise as new layers are added to the sequence. In fact modern noiseless digital tape recording goes a long way to avoiding noise build-up, but digital recorders with the right facilities for this type of recording are far too expensive for most of us to think seriously about buying one. The MIDI recording method will always be the more versatile of the two anyway, and any reasonably good quality recorder is all that is needed in order to produce tapes for others to listen to.

A sequencer that has a multi-tracking facility will almost certainly have a count-down facility that gives you a lead-in of so many beats before the sequence commences. This is better than operating the play control with your big-toe and commencing to play immediately! The more sophisticated systems enable recording to be started at any point in a sequence, so that you do not have to sit through 99 bars before playing a track that has only a few notes towards the end of a piece. This will work in conjunction with some sort of search command that moves to current position at a certain number of measures into the sequence.

The start, stop, and play instructions are self explanatory. Fast-forward and rewind are also very much like their tape recorder counterparts, but they usually play the sequence fast in the appropriate direction, and do not simply move the start position quickly backwards and forwards through the sequence. They are therefore more like the cue and review controls fitted on some tape recorders. They are perhaps more effective though, as the speeded-up MIDI sequence is not accompanied by the raising in pitch that occurs with speeded-up tape recordings. The only possible problem with this arrangement is that MIDI data might flow to the output at such a high rate that the data stream becomes overloaded, although the sequencer should avoid this by filtering any non-essential MIDI messages.

Other facilities
There is quite a range of facilities that can be incorporated in real-time sequencers. A common one is the ability to vary the tempo, so that (for instance) a difficult track can be recorded slowly and then boosted to the correct tempo. The ability to vary the overall playback speed of a piece is a standard feature, but some sequencers permit the speed to be changed at various points during the course of a piece. Of course, with multi-track tape recording, changing the playback speed is not an acceptable way of altering the tempo as it will also cause a change in pitch. MIDI recording is not hampered by this effect. A novel

method of setting the tempo on some sequencers is for a control button to be tapped at the desired beat rate.

Ideally a MIDI sequencer should enable 'program change' messages to be inserted at any desired points. Changing the program while recording a sequence may not be practicable, and the sequencer might filter out messages of this type anyway. Also, you might change your mind about the best program to use for part of a track. Track reassignment is a similar feature, but it enables a track to be switched to a different MIDI channel, to give a change in voice, or perhaps even a change to a different instrument. It might be possible to switch the instruments to provide the desired reassignment, but their channel assignment facilities might not be sufficiently flexible, and it would probably be easier to control things from the sequencer anyway.

Modular sequencing simply means creating short sequences that are then merged into a single piece. A 'transpose' facility is a very common one. In its basic form it affects all tracks, but some systems offer individual transpose facilities for each track. An offset or delay facility enables each track to be delayed slightly relative to the others. This could be used to produce some interesting chorus type effects, and it can also be used to iron out any lack of synchronization if some instruments in the system respond much less than instantly to received MIDI messages (a problem that I have not encountered in practice, but it apparently afflicts some instruments). A metronome facility provides an electronic equivalent to the old clockwork style metronome. Normally, when recording a new track on to existing tracks the system is arranged so that the player can hear the original tracks, and can keep in time with them. Where this is not possible a metronome facility may offer a relatively crude but effective alternative.

Memory gauge

Even with a modern 16 bit computer fitted with a large amount of memory there may still be a danger that a complex piece will use up all the memory. This will not necessarily cause the system to crash and lose all your data, but it is a great asset to have some form of memory indicator which gives an accurate indication of how much memory is left unused. You can then plan ahead and organize things so that optimum use is made of the memory. Specifications for MIDI sequencers indicate the amount of storage space for MIDI data in terms of MIDI 'events'. This is a slightly vague term, and if a sequencer can store 10000 events this does not mean it can handle up to 10000 notes. An event means a MIDI message, and as each note requires two messages (one to switch it on and the other to switch it off again), 10000 events means 5000 notes. Even this lower figure cannot be guaranteed, as there are likely to be other MIDI messages such as program changes. A few pitch bends could easily take several thousand events to complete! Although some sequencers may seem to offer a much higher storage capacity than you could ever need, this is not necessarily the case, and the larger the number of events that can be accommodated the better.

Track merging

A merge facility that enables two tracks to be combined into a single track is useful. For example, you might play parts on to different tracks, but then want to merge some of them in order to free tracks for further parts. With any fairly drastic editing of this type it is as well to remember that there may well be no easy way of reversing the process. Before utilizing any mass editing function it is a good idea to save the current version of a sequence to tape or disk. If anything goes drastically wrong, or you simply change your mind, you can then reload the unedited version of the sequence and try again. Some programs have an 'undo' facility, or a non-destructive editing mode. This effectively takes the back-up copy for you so that you can switch back to it if required. The copy may be held in RAM and not on tape or disk, so that changing back is virtually instant.

Filtering

MIDI filtering enables selected types of MIDI message to be ignored by the sequencer. There are two main applications for this feature, but you may well find other uses depending on how well (or otherwise) it is implemented on the system you use, and how complicated the setup happens to be. The main use for this feature is to filter out (during record) MIDI messages that would eat up too much memory. Possible candidates for elimination are aftertouch and pitch bend messages. Obviously some messages can be eliminated by playing the instrument in a way that does not generate memory consuming messages, but with messages such as aftertouch there may be no way of preventing the instrument from generating them.

A secondary use of filtering is to prevent clogging of the MIDI output data stream. If you build up a single piece from several complicated tracks there is a risk that the final sequence will require the transmission of more data than a single MIDI output can handle properly. Filtering out any non-essential data might then reduce the flow of data to an acceptable level. There are other possible uses if you get involved in swapping parts of sequences between one sequencer and another. As yet, this is not a particularly common way of working with MIDI, and is only applicable to a fairly sophisticated system anyway.

Any reasonably sophisticated sequencer should permit selected parts of a sequence be played back. By this I do not just mean it should be possible to jump to any point in a sequence, start playing back from there, and stop at the desired point. It should also be possible to playback only a certain track or tracks. Editing can be extremely difficult if there is no facility to isolate a single track.

Step-time sequencing

Step-time sequencing is a little more easily implemented than the real-time variety, and programs of this type generally offer a somewhat better range of features. In fact many of the facilities described above apply equally to step-time sequencing, but for software in a given price range there are likely to be more of them available on a step-time sequencer. Although there are numerous similarities between typical real and step-time sequencers, there are also some major differences to keep in mind.

In principle a step-time sequencer is very simple, and it is just a matter of having a program that enables note values and durations to be entered from the keyboard and stored in memory, with copying, deleting, and general modifying facilities being added. Real-time sequencers are usually organized into what are effectively two separate programs, with one being used for recording and playback, and the other providing the editing facilities. This approach is retained with some step-time types, although it is not really necessary to do things this way, and a single mode for entering and editing is preferable.

Step-time sequencing can be accomplished with the aid of a purely text display, or even with a very basic LED or liquid crystal display. However, it is something that people find vastly easier if a graphics display is used. A basic display may enable music to be entered quite easily, but it may also make it easy to make mistakes, and difficult to correct them. Even a fairly crude block graphics style display can make entering music and general editing tasks very much easier.

Final score
What are probably the ultimate in step-time sequencers are the 'scorewriter' or 'notation' programs as they are alternatively known. As explained previously, these use the computer's graphics to produce a representation of a stave, and notes etc. are entered onto this in con-

ventional music notation fashion. There are likely to be some aspects of standard music notation that are not implemented by each program of this type, but some have remarkably few limitations in this respect. The better programs can handle dotted notes, slurs, most dynamic markings, etc.

Like real-time sequencers, in the 'play' mode the timing can be altered to speed up or slow down the tempo to any desired degree (within reason). The ability to vary the tempo during the course of a piece is extremely useful with step-time sequencing. With real-time sequencing you can put in subtle changes of tempo to add expression to a piece simply by playing the music that way. With step-time sequencing these subtle changes must be programmed into the music. Some systems offer a 'randomize' facility which alters the timing of notes slightly so that they are not what could be called 'rhythm perfect'. This can make the music sound a little less mechanical, but it is unlikely to add genuine expression to a piece.

Comprehensive editing facilities are normally included so that wrong notes can be corrected, passages can be added or deleted, and any desired change can be made to a piece. The editing facilities usually include a comprehensive 'cut and paste' system, which enables blocks of music to be copied, moved or deleted. Shuffling data around in memory is one of the things that microprocessors do best, and that is really all these editing facilities amount to. There is no excuse for a step-time sequencer which does not let you manipulate the score in virtually any way you desire.

Standard MIDI files

All MIDI sequencers have the ability to save sequences on a floppy disk or cassette tape, but it is important to realise that they all save the data using a different method of coding. There may be some degree of compatibility between sequencer programs from the same software house, but in general data from one sequencer can not be read correctly into another sequencer. In order to overcome this problem the standard MIDI file was devised. This is a standard method of encoding/decoding track information, note data, etc., into a series of 8 bit codes which can be stored on any normal computer media, or sent via any normal computer interface. The idea is that sequencers should have the ability to produce and read in these files, so that they can be used with sequences produced on other sequencers. They can also produce standard files for use with any sequencer that can read this type of file.

This facility is an increasingly common one. It is certainly a feature that is offered by a number of ST sequencer programs, and some for other computers. When using it to swap sequences between ST programs I have never encounted any major problems. When trying to swap data between different computers there is a potential difficulty in that the two computers may not have the same disk size, or may not use the same format. With suitable software it should still be possible to swap the data via a standard interface such as an RS232C type, or MIDI come to that. Note that, as yet, MIDI does not include a facility specifically for interchanging these standard sequencer files.

Print it out

A useful feature of most notation programs, and one which is sufficient in itself to sell a lot of software of this type, is their ability to print out scores onto a suitable printer. The printer does not need to be a highly expensive type either, and most inexpensive dot-matrix types will provide quite good results. This facility enables the system to be used as what could be termed a 'note processor'. One word of warning though; there are a few notation programs which are only intended to be used in this way and which do not support MIDI, so make sure you know exactly what you are getting before you buy a notation program.

There should be some means of playing the instruments in the system from a step-time sequencer. Remember that there can only be one controller in a MIDI system at any one time. The instruments could be played via a keyboard instrument, with a switch being used to switch back and forth between the keyboard and the sequencer, as in Fig. 4.3. In fact this could be quite a good way of doing things, but many users would probably be quite happy with the simpler alternative of being able to play monophonically on any channel from the sequencer. The main use of this facility is when adjusting instruments for the correct sounds, and checking that they are all set up correctly. The problem with the arrangement of Fig. 4.3 is that the keyboard might not give access to every MIDI channel, and every voice of each instrument in the system. Many step-time sequencer systems consist of a computer plus a bank of rack-mount synthesizer and sampler modules. There may be no keyboard to play!

Real-and step-time sequencing combined

I suppose the obvious development is to combine real-time and step-time sequencing so that music can be entered either from the keyboard of an instrument, or from the computer keyboard, or from a combination of the two. The main advantage of step-time sequencing is that it enables music as complex as you like to be programmed, whether your playing ability is good, bad, or even totally non-existent. When played, a sequence will always be reproduced perfectly. The limiting factor is the composer's or arranger's imagination, not their playing ability. The two main drawbacks of this type of sequencing are that it can be relatively time consuming to enter a piece of music into the computer, and there is a lack of fine control over the final result. Some systems provide the option of several playing styles, but this is not as good as the precise control available with real-time sequencing.

A combination of the two systems gives the best of both worlds. Most users can quickly program large chunks of a piece exactly as they want them using the real-time capability, but the step-time facility is there for passages that go beyond the user's playing ability. The comprehensive editing facilities associated with step-time sequencers are there to be used regardless of which way the music was entered into the system. There is a definite trend towards this combining of the two types of sequencing, and many sequencers provide the two methods. However, as yet most programs seem to be heavily biased to one type or the other, and there seems to be little software available that manages to combine both systems really convincingly. For example, a notation program might be able to read in music from a keyboard instrument, but it might have difficulty in keeping up with more than the simplest of tracks. No doubt things will change before too long in this fast developing aspect of electronic music.

As a point of interest, step-time sequencing makes it possible to produce music that is unplayable in any other way, and some modern composers have adopted this method as their scores can not be played by even the most skilled musicians. This type of sequencing is not simply for those of limited playing ability, but also has the potential to break new ground.

The number of tracks you will require depends very much on the type of music you intend to produce, and while a 64 track sequencer may be very good for impressing your friends, few people would ever actually need this many. Most sequencers will handle at least 16 tracks, and this is sufficient for most needs. on the other hand, there are some sophisticated MIDI instruments around these days, and even quite a modest MIDI system could have sufficient hardware to merit more than 16 tracks. There are plenty of sequencers which offer 32, 64, or even higher numbers of tracks, and I suppose that with one of these there is little risk of you and your MIDI hardware outgrowing the software.

Some sequencers offer more tracks than there are MIDI channels, and is this achieved by assigning more than one track to some channels. Often you will wish to feed a single instrument with information from two tracks anyway (bass and treble parts for an electronic piano for instance). Even so, the number of MIDI channels might ultimately be the limiting factor, rather than the number of tracks supported by the sequencer. Some sequencers overcome this problem by having add-on multiple MIDI interfaces. The unit I use with an ST computer has three extra MIDI outputs that are totally independent of each other and the existing MIDI output. This gives four outputs with each one having its own set of 16 MIDI channels, giving some 64 independent MIDI channels in total! Even with quite a large system, this permits each channel of each instrument to have its own MIDI channel, giving maxium flexibility. Provided the computer and software can operate fast enough, having several independent MIDI outputs enables the system to cope better with large amounts of MIDI data. The timing of notes should be more accurate, and the risk of MIDI "choke" is reduced.

Voice editing/filing

A common complaint about many modern synthesizers and sound samplers is that they are difficult to program. Having an individual control for each parameter of each voice is not really practical, as today's multi-channel instruments would be so big that they would barely fit into an average size room. Perhaps the obvious way of reducing the number of controls to a manageable level would be to have a standard analogue synthesizer type control panel, plus a multi-way switch so that the controls could be assigned to each channel in turn.

Unfortunately, the instrument manufacturers seem to have streamlined things to a much greater degree, and current control panels generally consist of a single adjustable control knob plus a key-pad. The key-pad is used to select the desired voice and parameter, and then the knob is adjusted to set the parameter at the required level. In fact most recent instruments have done away with the control knob, and the key-pad is used to select the voice and parameter, and then to set the parameter at the desired figure. This helps to keep down the cost of sophisticated instruments, but it makes setting up a voice for precisely the required sound a very laborious process. Although a lot of instruments have a built-in disk drive or a cassette port that enables sets of voice parameters to be saved and reloaded, not all instruments have any form of program storage facility. Every parameter of every voice then has to be set up manually each time the instrument is used.

Many users do as little voice programming as possible, or even resign themselves to always using ready-programmed sounds.

With most MIDI equipped instruments the envelope shapers, filters, etc. can be set up via MIDI using controller messages. This opens up the possibility of using the computer both as a means of editing voice parameters more easily, and for storing sets of values. There are almost limitless ways of providing control via the computer, but for this sort of application a WIMP environment provides what is probably the best type of user interface (Fig. 4.7). A typical arrangement would have the computer's graphics providing an on-screen control panel complete with slider knobs and switches. The mouse and pointer would then be used to adjust these by positioning the pointer over the appropriate control knob, pressing a mouse button to 'hold' the 'knob', and then using the mouse to drag the 'knob' to its new position. As the parameters are varied, the new settings are transmitted to the instrument so that their effect can be heard and the settings can be easily fine-tuned.

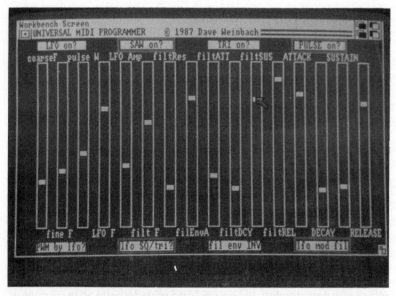

Figure 4.7 'Panel' is a general purpose MIDI program for the Amiga. It is set up here to act as a voice editor for the Sequential Circuits Six-Traks synth. The sliders and switches are controlled via the mouse and pointer

Save it

Having set up a voice correctly, the set of parameters can then be saved to tape or disk. They can then be reloaded whenever required, and then dumped to the instrument via MIDI. Computers save and load data under file names rather than numbers, which can make voice management very much easier. If you wish to load flute, guitar and string sounds, provided these sounds were saved under these names, they can be recalled using them. This is much easier than having to remember something like 12, 67 and 56, or use tables of sound types and numbers.

Some voice editing software provides even more help to the musician. A typical example would be where the envelope shapers are controlled by altering an on-screen diagram showing the envelope shape. The computer then translates the diagram into corresponding values for attack, sustain, etc., and transmits them to the instrument. This usually makes it very much easier to obtain the desired sound. Up-market instruments are fitted with disk drives that make it possible to quickly save and load programs, but there can still be advantages in using a computer for voice management.

Patch library software is similar to the voice type just described, but it uses system exclusive facilities (where available) to save and load complete sets of perhaps 100 or more programs. Where an instrument has an integral disk drive that provides this facility there is probably no point in using MIDI and a computer instead. It would almost certainly prove to be very much slower. However, many instruments have only a cassette interface or rely on relatively expensive program cartridges (which are a form of semiconductor memory). Some instruments have no facility for saving sets of programs other than via MIDI system exclusive messages. A computer equipped with a disk drive and suitable software can then be, to say the least, a great asset.

Sound samplers

Sound samplers deal with large amounts of data, and almost invariably have a built-in disk drive. They can still benefit from some of the types of software just described, and where it is possible to implement it, a visual editing system can be of great advantage. Sound samplers can operate by recording a complete sound and then simply playing it back (with or without any shift in pitch). This does not usually work very well in practice, except perhaps with percussion sounds. The problem is simply that a note of one length is recorded, but in use a note of virtually any duration might be required. Sound samplers overcome this problem by having what is effectively a standard synthesizer circuit, but with the sampling section replacing the VCOs of a conventional instrument. The recorded sample is usually just a short section from the beginning of a sound. It is converted into a continuous sound by looping back from near the end of the sample to an earlier point, and continuously playing this short section. Fig. 4.8 shows how this system of looping operates. The instrument's envelope shaper is used to provide an envelope which mimics that of the original sound, or to manipulate the sample in order to obtain a new sound.

Many instruments now provide a waveform display that can be used as an aid to selecting the right loop points (or they can be connected to a monitor that will provide such a display). This is a feature that is absent from many older samplers though. Where some form of built-in display is available, the higher resolution of a computer display could well offer a more accurate and convenient way of handling things. Using suitable loop points is essential, as there will otherwise be a serious glitch in the waveform that will produce an extremely rough sounding output. A good waveform display enables the optimum loop points to be located quickly and with certainty. A

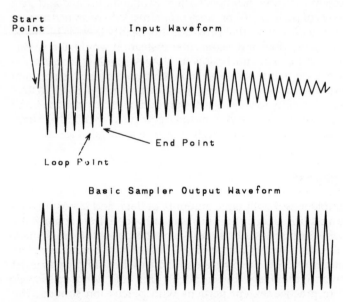

Figure 4.8 Selecting end and loop points using a visual editing system is child's play. Without one it is a matter of guesswork

visual editing system uses the computer's graphics capability to permit easy selection of the loop points. In order to work well this system requires a sophisticated link with the sampler via system exclusive messages, but most samplers can output sample dumps via MIDI, and permit loop points to be controlled by way of system exclusive or MIDI controller messages.

This covers the main types of software, but there are other types available. These include programs to help you home in on the desired sound or to generate exciting new sounds. The range of suitable software available depends on what computer and instruments you have, and it's a big advantage to have a computer and instrument that are popular for MIDI use (a Yamaha DX7 and an Atari ST for example).

5 MIDI equipment

The range of available MIDI equipment is probably larger than most people would imagine. Amongst other things, MIDI equipped guitars, mixers and effects units are all produced. There are also some relatively simple but useful MIDI accessories available. In this chapter we look at a wide range of devices, but as computers and software were dealt with in the previous chapter we will not consider these again here.

MIDI instruments

The fact that an instrument is excellent for conventional use does not necessarily mean that it will perform well in a MIDI context. A wide range of keyboard instruments which are equipped with a MIDI interface are currently available, including electronic organs, electronic pianos, and some up-market portable keyboards. However, there are still a great many instruments which do not support MIDI, although these are mainly small low cost types. An important point to keep in mind is that although a sophisticated instrument has MIDI sockets, it may not have a particularly impressive MIDI implementation. Some instruments which pre-date MIDI were brought out in later versions which provided MIDI operation, but had gaps in their MIDI specification. As an example, some of these instruments have touch sensitive keyboards and respond to velocity information received via MIDI, but do not transmit velocity information when the keyboard is played. With instruments brought out in the early days of MIDI, the MIDI interface and software was added as something of an after-thought, and again, the specification was less impressive than the general sophistication of these instruments might lead one to expect.

As MIDI has grown in importance, and a good MIDI implementation has become a strong selling point, gaps in the specification have largely been bridged. There are still some quite expensive instruments which do not quite live up to expectations, and a lack of mode 4 is a common omission. With something like an electronic piano mode 4 would be pointless, since each voice provides the same sound. Mode 4 is often absent with sound samplers that, on the fact of it, would seem able to implement this mode and provide excellent results.

Some sound samplers provide multi-timbral operation via a splitting system rather than by assigning different sounds to different MIDI channels. This is quite a good system for samplers, as the range of notes available from a single sample is usually quite limited when compared to the compass of a synthesizer. Even if a single sample could be stretched over a very wide range of notes, at the extremes of the range the quality of the sound would almost certainly leave a lot to be desired.

The splits
A system of keyboard splitting enables a low pitched sample to be assigned to the lower section of the keyboard, and a higher pitched sample to be assigned to the upper section. This permits a wider compass to be accommodated, with a good quality sound over the full range (see Fig. 5.1). Keyboard split arrangements seem to become ever more versatile as new instruments are introduced, and it is possible to split the keyboard into three or more sections in some cases. You can have something like a five part percussion section provided by a single sound sampler occupying a single MIDI channel.

The split operation should still work when an instrument is controlled via MIDI, with ranges of notes being assigned to a certain voice of the instrument. Although designed primarily to give more consistent results over a wide range of notes, the samples used can be totally

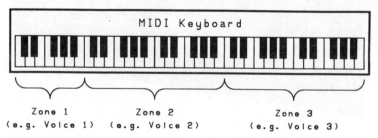

Figure 5.1 Most MIDI keyboards permit a system of zoning such as this

different if desired. With a suitable instrument this permits several sounds to be independently controlled, giving something which is close to mode 4 operation. It is inferior to mode 4 operation in that instruments can be independently controlled only if they cover separate ranges of notes. It is superior to mode 4 operation in that it gives a form of multi-channel operation but occupies only a single MIDI channel. Split operation is also superior in that polyphonic sequencing is possible, whereas mode 4 is strictly one note per channel. An instrument which has a sophisticated mode of this type is a valuable asset in a MIDI setup, although I suppose that for optimum flexibility it should offer mode 4 as well as and not instead of split keyboard operation.

Rack-mounted instruments

Finding space for a number of keyboard instruments can be quite difficult, and in a MIDI context one keyboard per instrument is not usually justified. In a system which has several keyboard instruments the cost of the excess keyboards could run into hundreds of pounds. The manufacturers' answer to this problem is rack-mounting versions of many of their more popular up-market instruments. These have no keyboard, and fit into a standard 19 inch wide rack (see Fig. 5.2). Most units are only 3.5 inches tall, and a stack of half a dozen rack-mount instruments will easily fit onto an average desk, leaving plenty of space to one side for other equipment. An interesting point to note about some of these rack mount instruments is that they are not just a keyboard instrument minus the keyboard. Some are given extra features that make them more attractive for MIDI use, and this can range

Figure 5.2 Yamaha's TG77 is essentially the rack mount version of the SY77 synthesiser

from something as simple as including a MIDI THRU socket that is absent on the keyboard version, to something more substantial such as adding an implementation of mode 4. There seem to be a few instruments now that were designed from the outset as modules for MIDI control, and which have no true keyboard equivalents.

Apart from the ability to produce good sounds, probably the most important assets for MIDI instruments are the inclusion of both modes 3 and 4 (preferably plus some form of multi mode), and the implementation of at least basic touch sensitivity (i.e. the instrument should transmit/receive velocity information, and preferably some form of aftertouch information as well). A lot of low cost keyboard instruments appear to be ideal for MIDI use, but a close examination of their specification often reveals a lack of at least one of these criteria. Modern keyboard instruments are generally much better in this respect than those of a few years ago. A less than ideal instrument at a low price is an attractive proposition for someone putting together a budget MIDI system, and will probably perform quite well. On the other hand, it can be frustrating to (say) program a piece with carefully controlled dynamics that are ignored by most of the instruments during playback.

Check your specs
Always check MIDI specification sheets very carefully. Apart from looking to see if there are any glaring omissions in the specification, there may be some extras that are of value for MIDI control. In particular, some modern instruments have about 16 to 32 voices plus sophisticated multi modes that enable them to be used where it might otherwise require two or three instruments to gives the same effect.

If you are contemplating the purchase of a secondhand instrument, do not assume that its MIDI specification will be the same as current instruments of the same type. Modern instruments are frequently updated, and quickly become outdated. Often an upgrade is available, and this might just involve changing an integrated circuit inside the unit, or with a disk based instrument it might only be necessary to use a new disk when starting up the instrument. However, where an instrument has been upgraded several times, or has been the subject of major revision, there may be no way of upgrading an early example to the current specification. When buying second-hand you need to check carefully to determine exactly what you are buying, and whether any necessary upgrade is actually available.

Integral sequencers
MIDI instruments often feature built-in sequencers of one kind or

another. These can be useful, and modern instruments tend to have much more sophisticated sequencers than those in the early days of MIDI. If you require a sequencer, but do not wish to go the whole way with a computer based system, a good integral type will almost certainly represent the most cost effective solution. However, few give anything approaching the level of performance possible with sequencers based on personal computers, and you might soon outgrow even one of the better integral types.

MIDI keyboards

Few MIDI systems are totally devoid of a keyboard, although this is quite feasible if your only interest is step-time sequencing, or if a guitar or some other forms of controller will be used. For most purposes the keyboard of a good touch sensitive synthesizer or sound sampler will be adequate. If you have a MIDI equipped electronic piano in your setup, then this may well be a good choice as the main MIDI keyboard. Electronic pianos usually have excellent keyboards from the playing point of view. For MIDI operation their wide compass (seven octaves on many electronic pianos) and sophisticated touch sensitivity make them difficult to better provided the MIDI implementation is reasonably complete.

Figure 5.3 Roland's JX-1 entry level synth

Another option is to buy a purpose built MIDI keyboard. In other words, a keyboard that only provides MIDI messages, and has no built-in sound generation circuits of any type. These vary enormously in the degree of sophistication they offer, and in price. In the likely event that an instrument in the system has a reasonably good keyboard and MIDI support for it, there is little point in obtaining anything other than a fairly sophisticated keyboard. This should offer a compass of at least five octaves, touch sensitivity (preferably including some sort of after-touch), and some form of split keyboard operation. In this context, split keyboard operation means the ability to divide the keyboard into zones, with each zone being assigned to a different MIDI channel. This enables the left and right hands to play different instruments, or different channels of the same instrument. Some keyboards provide a three-way split, and most that have a split feature enable the user to define the zones (although zones might have to be complete octaves).

MIDI keyboards sometimes have facilities for sending MIDI messages such as program selection, mode change, and timing messages. This type of thing can be useful, especially in a system that is based on the keyboard rather than a computer plus sequencer software.

MIDI expander

MIDI expanders are aimed primarily at electronic organ players. They are used in the manner shown in Fig. 5.4 and the basic idea is for the expander to provide a range of (usually) preset sounds to augment

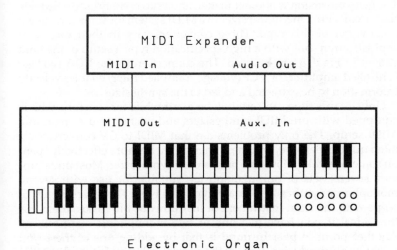

Figure 5.4 A MIDI expander is intended primarily for use in this fashion

103

those available on the organ. With a MIDI equipped electronic organ that has twin keyboards, it is usually possible to assign each one to a different channel, and with a suitable expander each keyboard can then play a different voice of the expander. Units of this type are polyphonic, and would typically give up to eight notes at once (four per channel if used in the two voice mode). A MIDI expander could be used in any MIDI system, and not just as a simple add-on for an electronic organ. With one or two exceptions, MIDI expanders seem to be little used other than by organists. If you can tolerate the limited control over the sound generator circuits (or the convoluted access via MIDI rather than front panel controls that some units offer), the better of the expanders offer what is probably the least expensive way to substantially enhance a MIDI system.

MIDI to CV converter

With a lot of musicians having spent large sums of money on synthesizers in the pre-MIDI days, there is naturally a lot of interest in updating instruments with the old gate/CV method of control to MIDI operation. It is technically quite possible to provide CV/gate to MIDI conversion, but this would give what would probably be a rather crude MIDI controller. It is doubtful if this type of conversion unit would be worthwhile, and I have not encountered one. MIDI to CV/gate conversion is another matter, and I successfully used a Sequential Circuits Pro One synthesizer in a MIDI system for some time using a converter of this type. These converters vary in their degree of sophistication, but with a high specification type a setup of the kind shown in Fig. 5.5 can be used. The connection to the VCA (voltage controlled amplifier) or VCF (voltage controlled filter) enables velocity information to be extracted and fed to the synthesizer.

Units of this type can certainly be worthwhile for someone who is equipped with pre-MIDI synthesizers and wishes to use them in a MIDI setup. The only problems are that MIDI to CV converters are often quite expensive, and the money might be more effectively spent on something like a low cost rack-mount synthesizer. Most units provide several sets of outputs, and are suitable for use with several monophonic synthesizers or a polyphonic type. This gives plenty of scope with the right instrument or instruments, but makes them less than ideal if you have just one or two monophonic synthesizers. Another point to bear in mind is that by adding one of these you might be reintroducing some of the compatibility problems that MIDI was supposed to solve!

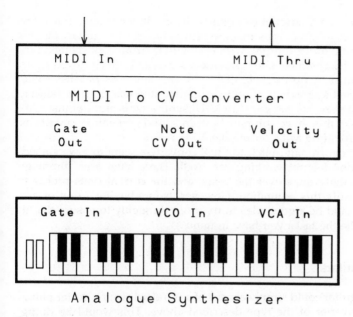

Figure 5.5 Some MIDI/CV converters use this arrangement to give velocity control

Pitch to MIDI converter

For keyboard players MIDI is no problem as there are countless MIDI keyboard instruments available. For guitarists and others, things are decidedly less rosy. One solution to the problem is a pitch to MIDI converter, and this is a device which analyses the audio input signal from an instrument, and generates the appropriate MIDI note on and note off messages. This may not sound too difficult, but it is not easy to produce a system of this type that works well. Apart from getting the pitch tracking accurate with a wide range of input waveforms, and detecting the beginnings and ends of notes properly with a wide variety of envelope shapes, there can also be slight but noticeable delays. The input signal has to be sampled for a number of cycles in order to accurately determine its pitch, and this inevitably takes a significant time.

Units of this type are relatively rare, and could be quite expensive if you do manage to track one down. They permit virtually any instrument (or even the human voice) to be used as a MIDI controller, since the input signal can be derived via a microphone and amplifier with

105

non-electronic instruments. Some units are monophonic, but there are also polyphonic units that are primarily aimed at guitarists. The latter can be multi-timbral, with each guitar string controlling a different MIDI channel. They provide what is only likely to be quite crude control by up-market MIDI keyboard standards, but they could still be used to good effect with a sophisticated real-time sequencer. Some units in this category are MIDI synthesizers and not just converters (i.e. they have complex built-in sound generation circuits as well as providing MIDI output data).

Rightly or wrongly, pitch to MIDI converters seem to have gained a reputation for not working very well. There have been improvements in these units over the years, and the current units probably do not justify this reputation. However, before buying a unit of this type it would be a good idea to try it out throughly to ensure that it can handle the tasks you have in mind.

MIDI guitars

A MIDI guitar could simply consist of a standard electric guitar plus a pitch converter of the type described above. This would be doing things the hard way though, and more accurate and sophisticated control can be obtained by building sensors into the guitar to detect which note or notes are being played. A system of this type avoids the delays associated with pitch conversion devices. This basic idea of 'wiring' a guitar so that its fretboard operates rather like a conventional keyboard is not exactly new, and I seem to remember a guitar in the 1960s which could be played simply by fingering notes without actually plucking them.

Most modern MIDI guitars make these early instruments look quite crude by comparison. A typical specification would include the transmission of velocity information, mode 4 operation with each string being assigned to a different channel, pressure sensors to operate the desired MIDI controllers (filter cutoff frequency, filter resonance, or whatever), and a digital display to help set up everything as desired. With some recently introduced low cost instruments the world of MIDI will now be accessible to a great many more musicians, and this could give further impetus to the growth in the popularity of MIDI. A conventional guitar plus a whole bank of effects units would certainly seem to be very much second best when compared with a MIDI guitar plus any reasonably competent MIDI synthesizer. Guitarists no longer need to be jealous of the range of sounds available to keyboard players.

Figure 5.6 The Roland GK-2 MIDI controller

Wind synthesis

It would presumably be possible to apply the MIDI guitar idea to any musical instrument, and this has also been applied to wind instruments. These can be quite refined, and apart from producing basic MIDI note on and note off information with the appropriate note values, velocity information can be derived via a breath sensor. There can even be pressure sensors in the mouthpiece to provide control of pitch bend or whatever.

This is again not a totally new idea, and electronic breath controlled instruments have been produced in the past. They have never caught on in a big way, but with the advantages that MIDI provides it is possible that this new breed of wind instrument will become a standard form of electronic instrument in the near future.

Drum pads

Electronic drum kits have been around for many years, and a set of drum pads that provide MIDI output signals is a natural progression from these. There are two ways in which a set of MIDI drum pads can be used. The obvious way is to connect the output to a MIDI instrument which then provides the required sounds. This is a versatile arrangement as it can provide a vast range of sounds in addition to the standard percussion repertoire. The usual setup would be to have each pad assigned to a different MIDI channel, and to use the synthesizer or other instrument in mode 4 so as to obtain a different sound from each pad. An alternative is to have all the pads assigned to the same channel, but to have each one produce a different note. This can be used to good effect with an instrument that can assign each voice to a particular note. This is the way MIDI drum machines operate, and it is also possible with some other instruments (the Ensoniq Mirage sound sampler for example). With a suitable instrument it is effectively the same as using mode 4.

The second way of using drum pads is when programming drum parts into a real-time sequencer. For an experienced drummer this offers a much better way of doing things than tapping rhythms on to keys of a keyboard instrument, especially when sequencing complex patterns.

Drum machines

MIDI includes the timing information needed by drum machines in the form of the clock, song position, and other system timing messages. Most MIDI sequencers can transmit and (or) recognize these timing messages, and so MIDI equipped drum machines can be readily integrated into most MIDI systems. As explained previously, for external triggering/programming the standard system of drum assignment is to match the drum sounds to different notes. There is no true standard method of assigning particular drum sounds to specific notes (although some conventions are emerging), and some machines offer the flexibility of being able to assign any drum to any desired note. It is unusual for drum machines to implement MIDI mode 4, with each drum assigned to a different MIDI channel. This would not really be a very good way of handling things, as it would eat up a fair proportion of the available channels. With the matching of drums and notes it is possible to sequence the drums in any required fashion, but only a single MIDI channel needs to be occupied if mode 3 is selected.

Most drum machines are programmed by way of touch pads that are really just simple on/off switches, and these do not provide touch sensitivity. However, if a drum machine is programmed via its MIDI input and a touch sensitive keyboard or drum pad, the MIDI velocity information will usually be stored and used by the instrument.

Mixers

Audio mixers might not seem like ideal candidates for the MIDI treatment, but a few devices of this type are available. One way of implementing MIDI control of mixers would be to assign the faders to variable MIDI controllers. This would enable very fine and sophisticated control, but it has a definite drawback. This is simply that about the only way of controlling such a unit properly would be with the aid of a computer plus some elaborate software. It would also require large amounts of MIDI data to be transmitted at times, which could lead to clogging up of the system.

A more fundamental but practical approach is usually adopted, and this makes use of MIDI program change messages. The idea is to store sets of fader adjustments as programs, and then to call up each set of adjustments as it is required. This is a relatively crude way of tackling things in that it gives what in practice would have to be a series of large jumps in the setting of each fader. This can still be quite useful. In its favour, this system requires the transmission of minimal amounts of MIDI data, and a wide range of MIDI controllers can be used to provide program change messages. It also makes it quite quick and easy to set up and use the equipment.

MIDI pedals

MIDI pedals are used to transmit pitch bend or controller information. A crucial point to remember here is that there can only be one controller in a MIDI system. Therefore, these would normally be used only for a live performance. In other words, when playing a keyboard instrument, a foot pedal could be used to provide pitch bend or to control some other parameter, but it would not be possible to use a MIDI sequencer at the same time in order to provide an automatic backing track (although a sequencer built into the instrument could probably be used to do this).

MIDI merge units

In fact it is not strictly true to say that there can only be one controlling device in a MIDI system, as there is actually a way of using two controllers. This requires the use of a MIDI mixer, but by this I mean a unit which mixes the two signals into a single data stream, rather than a MIDI controlled audio mixer (as described above). Devices of this type are sometimes called MIDI 'merge' units. I suppose that it would be possible to synchronize two MIDI sequencers, and to combine their outputs using a MIDI merge unit. This is doing things the hard way though, and it would probably be possible to program the entire sequence into one of the more capable MIDI sequencers. If a piece can not be handled by one of the better MIDI sequencers, then it is quite possible that the amounts of data involved would overload the MIDI channel anyway.

A more likely use for a MIDI merge unit is in a setup of the type shown in Fig. 5.7. Here a set of MIDI drum pads and a sequencer are used as the controllers. This permits the use of a sophisticated external sequencer to provide an accompaniment for the keyboard player, but it also enables the drum pads to exploit some otherwise unused channels of the synthesizer.

MIDI merge units do not seem to be particularly common MIDI accessories, and are a lot more complex than a basic two or three channel audio mixer. The signals are not being mixed together in quite the same way as mixing audio signals. Once the unit has started accepting a MIDI message on one input, it must feed this through to the output. Any message received on another input during this period must be stored in a block of memory (called a buffer), and then transmitted

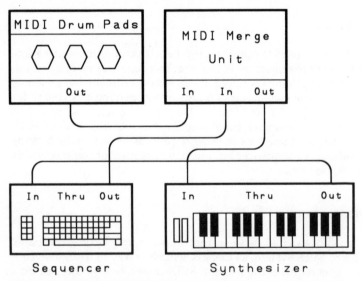

Figure 5.7 A MIDI merge unit enables two controllers to be used (drum pads and a sequencer in this example)

when the original message has finished. System timing messages must be fed straight through to the output, in the middle of other messages if necessary, but the system must still deal in complete bytes and not muddle part of one byte into another. This requires the use of a microprocessor based circuit, and this takes MIDI merge units out of the very inexpensive accessory class.

A MIDI merge unit is probably an accessory that is of more use to some doing live performances than to a MIDI studio user, and is something few users really need. One of these could be of tremendous value in the right circumstances though.

MIDI switch

A MIDI merge unit could be used in a situation where you wish to control the system from a sequencer for most of the time, but will occasionally need to control it from a MIDI keyboard. This is a convenient way of handling things in that you can use one or the other without needing to alter any controls, but it is a rather expensive solution to the problem. A much cheaper method is to use a MIDI switch, which connects one unit or the other through to the output, under the control of a manually operated switch. If you are handy with a soldering iron there should be little difficulty in putting together your own MIDI switch. Fig. 5.8 shows the simple wiring involved (the switch is any DPDT type, such as a slider or miniature toggle switch). Some commercial units provide several outputs, not just two. For most purposes a simple two output type is sufficient though.

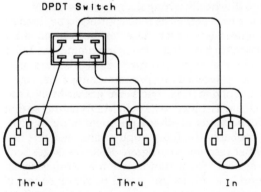

Figure 5.8 The wiring of a MIDI switch is very simple, and can be put together by an average DIY enthusiast

Effects units

Effects units that permit MIDI control are mostly types that are based on digital delay lines. These provide chorus, flanging, echo, etc. The ability to control the type of effect obtained via MIDI is a very useful one. Apart from obvious application in a studio setup, it can also be a major asset for live performances. A MIDI sequencer can be used to provide an automatic backing, and (if it is a suitable type) it can also be programmed to give the required effects changes automatically.

Effects unit control can be implemented via MIDI controller messages, but as with audio mixers, it is more normal to use program select messages. This method works better than it does with audio mixers, since an effects unit often just provides a series of preset effects. Where fine control of an individual effect is possible (flanging depth for example), this would normally be preset at the level required by the user, and would not be varied in mid-performance. The ability to make programmed fine adjustments to effects would certainly be quite useful, but it would require the use of specialized MIDI software, and its absence is something that few people are likely to miss.

Of course, it is up to the user to check the specification sheet for the effects unit, and to ensure that the correct program select messages for the required effects are sent by the sequencer. There is no standardization of effects and their corresponding program numbers. Where effects are user adjustable, it is up to the user to ensure that each effect is set up correctly before starting a performance. This type of thing enables very professional and well produced music to be produced by a reasonably skilful player, but the setting up must always be done meticulously. It can all go drastically wrong if a mistake is made!

It is quite common for effects as well as tone controls to be fitted to guitar amplifiers, and with a few units these can be controlled by MIDI messages. This works in essentially the same manner as MIDI control of effects units, with the required control settings being stored as MIDI programs, and then selected using program change messages.

There are two basic ways of handling effects changes via MIDI. One way is to have the effects unit assigned to its own MIDI channel so that it can be controlled independently of other equipment in the system. The second method is probably the more popular one, and this has the effects unit or amplifier respond to program select messages sent to instruments in the system. For instance, when a synthesizer is changed to a string sound, the effects unit would be set up so that it would use this program change message to switch to a chorus effect. But what if you sometimes require the effect to change, but not the sound from the instrument? This can be accommodated by this system with most instruments, and it is merely a matter of assigning the same set of control parameters to more than one program. You can then match one basic sound with several effects. This system has its limitations, but it is flexible enough for most users.

Filtering

MIDI filtering does not mean a MIDI controlled audio filter, but a device that will selectively remove MIDI messages. In the past the instrument manufacturers have tended to carefully design MIDI implementations so that a slave instrument can exactly mimic the master instrument. This is not necessarily a particularly useful arrangement, as in most cases the slave instrument is required to do something substantially different from the master. Simply having the slave mimic the master does not, to myself at any rate, seem to be particularly useful.

It is noticeable that on most of the more recently introduced instruments the MIDI implementation gives quite good control over what MIDI messages are transmitted and recognized. this is built-in filtering, and is an extremely useful feature. For example, you might require the slave instrument to produce the same sounds throughout a piece, and would then not want the slave instrument to respond to MIDI program change messages. This can be achieved if either the master can be set not to transmit program change messages, or the slave instrument can be set to ignore them.

Where suitable built-in filtering is not available, an external unit connected between the master and slave instruments can do the job. A unit of this type is potentially very useful indeed, but such a device could be difficult to track down. I have seen it suggested that an external MIDI filter unit can be used to reduce clogging of the data stream during periods of high activity, such as when pitch bend information is being transmitted. This should certainly be possible with built-in filtering, but it is difficult to see how it could be effective with an external unit. The input data stream would become clogged causing delays and (or) lost data. There is no way MIDI filters can reinstate lost data, or transmit data before it has been received. An external filter could be used to remove pitch bend information in order to reduce the amount of data being fed to a sequencer, so as to conserve memory.

There is a form of MIDI filter called a 'channel filter', and this filters out all MIDI channel messages that are not on a particular MIDI channel. Some MIDI equipment will only work in the omni mode, and will therefore respond to any recognized messages regardless of what channel they are on. A MIDI channel filter effectively converts an omni mode device to poly mode operation.

A channel filter should not be confused with a so-called 'channelizer'. The latter is intended for use with a MIDI instrument that transmits on channel 1 (something of a rarity these days, but some early MIDI instruments were restricted in this way). The channelizer takes in the MIDI messages, and transmits them with a new channel number in place of the original. This effectively enables the instrument to transmit information on any channel.

Sequencers

A MIDI sequencer does not necessarily mean a home or personal computer running a sequencer program, or a sequencer that is built into an instrument. Stand-alone sequencers are available, and these are mostly designed along pseudo multi-track tape recorder lines. Some also offer step-time sequencing (or possibly only step-time sequencing). These stand-alone units do not seem to have achieved great popularity, and the inclusion of built-in sequencers on so many synthesizers and sound samplers is probably a contributory factor. Stand-alone units are generally easier to use than built-in sequencers, with a higher specification as well (more channels, note capacity, etc.). They tend to be quite expensive though, and this does not make them an attractive proposition to someone who has an instrument with a built-in sequencer. Also, a personal computer plus suitable software could well give a vastly superior sequencer at a comparable price. The computer can be used for games, word processing, etc., but a stand-alone MIDI sequencer is strictly that.

Sync units

The most simple type of MIDI synchronization unit is one that converts conventional drum machine clock signals into MIDI timing signals. A conversion in the opposite direction is also possible, with MIDI timing messages being converted into conventional clock signals. How well this type of arrangement does, or does not work out in practice is very much dependent on the particular items of equipment used, and the sophistication of the converters.

A relatively new type of MIDI converter is the SMPTE synchronization unit. SMPTE is the standard system of synchronization used by professional studios that utilize video or film equipment. This system is very simple in essence. Each frame carries timing codes which indicate how far into the sequence that particular frame is. This is done on the basis of hours, minutes, seconds, frames, and sub-frames (for added precision, each frame is divided into 80 sub-frames). This timing information can be decoded and then re-encoded into MIDI song pointer messages. This could be used, for example, when making a recording of an SMPTE encoded tape of acoustic instruments into which a MIDI sequence must be integrated. This type of thing is of great benefit to many professional users, but probably few amateur musicians will ever wish to mix SMPTE and MIDI equipment.

Other ideas

There seems to be an ever growing list of MIDI accessories and larger items of equipment, and there must be almost endless possibilities. There are units that use infra-red or radio waves to give a cordless MIDI link between items of equipment, and devices that provide operation over more than the guaranteed MIDI maximum of 15 metres. Note though, that any links which use radio signals might be illegal to operate (or even illegal to buy).

Sound-to-light units normally operate by having a microphone that picks up the music, or an audio input that is fed with the music signal. A MIDI-to-light unit could work in a similar way, but by converting MIDI messages into suitable light control signals. Another possibility would be to control a lighting unit using program change messages, in much the same way that mixers and effects units are controlled.

Personal computers equipped with disk drives are often used to store program data and other data used by instruments. This is quite a good system if the computer will also be used for sequencing, but it is a pretty expensive solution if it will only be used for voice filing and the like. The obvious alternative is to have a MIDI data filer unit consisting of a disk drive plus some interfacing and control circuits. This could potentially do the job very well at a relatively low cost. As yet this type of equipment does not seem to be particularly common, but with the increasing complexity of modern instruments a built-in disk drive or external filer unit could become virtually essential. Add-on disk drive units seem to be dedicated types (i.e. only suitable for one particular instrument or range of instruments), and the extensive use of system exclusive messages for voice filing and other data storage and retrieval could make a universal MIDI data filer difficult to produce, although Yamaha have attempted this with the MFD1.

MIDI could have been tailor-made for imaginative add-ons, and no doubt some interesting new accessories will emerge over the next few years. In particular, units that take the MIDI output signal from a keyboard and process it in some way before it is fed to a synthesizer module could take off in a big way (MIDI harmonizers for example).

6 MIDI music

I suppose that this should be the longest chapter in this book. The only reason that it is not is that in the previous discussion of the MIDI language, equipment, etc. we have already covered a number of ways in which MIDI equipment can be formed into systems that permit effective music making. In this chapter we will fill in some of the gaps left by the earlier chapters, recapitulate to some extent, and suggest ways of designing a system to suit your needs.

An important point to realize with modern developments in computing, including MIDI, is that they will not do your thinking for you. In a MIDI context, a superb electronic music system is not going to turn you into a great composer, arranger, or player. What MIDI can do is enable you to experiment and realize your ideas much more easily than has been possible in the past. Large scale compositions and arrangements can be played by a computer based MIDI system – you no longer need to hire a band or orchestra! The reproduced music may in some cases lack the musicianship of a real band or orchestra, but it does at least enable you to hear the music, learn from your mistakes, and perfect each piece. What is perhaps the greatest advantage of a MIDI system is the speed with which you can learn when using it. It can help you to reach standards that you might otherwise never achieve.

Using a real-time sequencer it is possible to build up a complex multi-track piece and, provided you have the playing skills, have the piece exactly as you want it. This type of thing has been possible in the past, but only for those with access to extremely expensive studio equipment. MIDI brings this type of thing within the range of practically everyone, and it offers greater versatility than previous recording methods. Even if your playing skills are sometimes a bit rough at the edges, a system with suitable editing facilities will enable you to 'massage' the stored data to give an acceptable final result. Provided you can supply the ideas and basic skills, MIDI will enable you to make the most of them.

Basic systems

Having reached this far you should be familiar with chaining MIDI equipment together, the star method of connection, MIDI merge units, and MIDI switches. Presumably you will also be familiar with the MIDI operating modes and messages. It will be assumed here you are conversant with all these topics, and you need to do some further study of the earlier chapters if you are not. These are all essential knowledge for anyone who is going to use MIDI effectively.

The first step in putting together a MIDI system is to decide exactly what you want to do with it. A system based on a computer running a score-writer program and having a printer plus a bank of rack-mount synthesizers is great for composers and arrangers, but is likely to be practically useless for an avid keyboard player. Probably many MIDI users are keyboard players who regard MIDI as a way of providing a more powerful system than can be provided by a single instrument. This is certainly a valid use of MIDI, but as keyboard instruments become more and more capable, the advantages of adding more synthesizers, sound samplers, of whatever, gradually diminishes, unless you can muster a total of more than ten fingers and thumbs.

If we start with systems of this type, simply chaining together a series of keyboard instruments, or a mixture of keyboard instruments and rack-mount types, might not give a usable setup. This is where MIDI modes and channels are usually all-important, and a keyboard that can provide split operation is more than a little helpful. Using the most basic arrangement, two instruments would be used to give thicker sounds, with all voices on the first instrument set to give one sound, and all the voices of the second instrument set to give another sound. The two audio output signals would have to be mixed and then fed to an amplifier, or they could be sent to separate amplifiers. With this arrangement MIDI mode 1 is sufficient. No matter what channel the master instrument sends notes on, the slave instrument will play them.

Quick change
This arrangement can be improved by the use of program change messages, if the master instrument has some means of transmitting them. In practice a change of program is almost invariably accompanied by the automatic transmission of a program change message.

This feature can often be enabled and disabled via some form of front panel switching, and the default mode may well be for no program change messages to be sent. This can be useful, as you may want to change the program on the master without the slave program being changed. If the slave instrument can be set to ignore program change messages, the same result can be achieved by setting it to this mode of operation. A feature that is becoming increasing common is the ability to change to a new program, but to have a different program number in the transmitted MIDI program change message. This can make it easier to pair the sounds on the master instrument with those on the slaves.

Changing the program running on the slave without altering the program on the master is a bit more tricky. Most instruments can only send a program change message if their own program is altered. One way of achieving the desired result, and probably the only way, is to set the master instrument so that two programs are identical, but to set the slave unit so that its equivalent programs are different. Changing from one program to the other on the master then gives no change in its sound, but the change of program on the slave will do so. This type of thing obviously takes a little preplanning and preparation, but so do simple pairs of programs. It is up to the user to ensure that each program on the master is properly matched to the required program (and therefore sound) on the slave instrument.

Null programs

A similar technique that might prove useful is to have a 'null' program on one of the instruments. In other words, have the parameters of a program set so that it does not produce any sound. This can be achieved with most instruments, although you might need to experiment a little in order to find a setup that gives the desired effect. It might be possible to achieve zero output simply by switching off all the signal sources, or perhaps by using appropriate envelope shaper parameters, or setting the filter for zero cutoff frequency. One of the MIDI controllers is often an overall volume control, and setting this to zero should have the desired effect.

The point of a null program is that it enables you to effectively switch off one or other of the instruments during passages where only one instrument is required. A simple on/off switch connected in one of the wires of the MIDI lead (as in Fig. 6.1) can achieve much the same effect, and could be a convenient way of doing things if the switch is a foot operated type. This method is a little more limited in that it can only mute the slave instrument, and it is not possible to play on the keyboard of the master instrument while having only the slave actu-

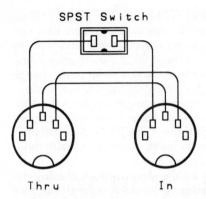

SPST Switch

Thru   In

Figure 6.1 A MIDI on/off switch is another simple device

ally producing any sound. Also, the switch must be used carefully to avoid cutting out any note off messages that would leave notes playing on the slave.

Although we are only talking in terms of two instruments here, there is no problem in having several instruments in the system, with each one set up to provide the right program (including null types) as program change messages are received from the master instrument. Whether this would be worthwhile is another matter. It is something that is more likely to be worthwhile with a keyboard that is capable of split (MIDI channel) operation, or where the slave instrument(s) can provide split (note range) operation. With the latter, mode 1 operation will still probably suffice. In a very basic setup the single slave instrument would have a keyboard split to match the master instrument, but with suitable instruments it might be possible to set up something a little more exotic. If the slave instrument can be set up to produce certain percussion sounds when particular notes a.e played, it might be possible to set (say) the lowest octave on the master instrument's keyboard to a null program, and then to use this octave to control a slave instrument set to provide a drum set. Whether or not this sort of thing is possible depends very much on the particular instruments you are using, and some in-depth reading of manuals and careful planning is required when you start trying to stretch the capabilities of a system to the limits.

A keyboard which provides zones that can be assigned to MIDI channels gives greater possibilities. Again, you could have the lowest octave of the keyboard to provide a drum set on a slave instrument, with the rest of the keyboard split into two halves and controlling two instruments set to give different sounds. This can give complete isolation between the instruments, with no risk of unwanted bass notes

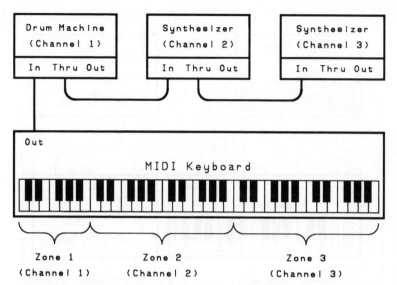

Figure 6.2 A keyboard which provides zones is very powerful in combination with mode 3 instruments

being played along with the drums. This really requires the use of a separate MIDI keyboard though, or a keyboard instrument set to the local off mode so that it acts as a separate keyboard and sound generator module. Fig. 6.2 shows how such a system might be organized.

Effects

With MIDI compatible effects units it should be easy to provide changes in effects at the required times. Fig. 6.3 shows how a two instrument and two effects unit system could be arranged. This is essentially the same as the twin instrument arrangement discussed earlier, and the two instruments would be used in the same way, with program change messages being used to change their sounds as and when required. However, the effects units would also be programmed to respond to these messages, giving the required switches in the effects. The ability to program a series of effects in advance and then call them up automatically when they are required is one that should not be underestimated. Once again though, meticulous planning and setting up is essential if it really is 'going to be all right on the night'.

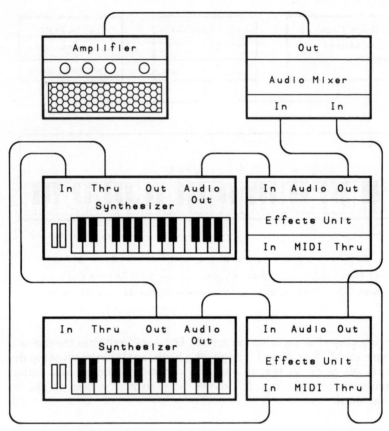

Figure 6.3 MIDI effects units can be connected in the system and controlled via program change messages

Do not fall into the trap of thinking that because everything in a system has MIDI sockets, it all has to be connected up as one big MIDI system. In most cases this is indeed the best way of doing things, but it is not necessarily the best method in all circumstances. Fig. 6.4 shows two synthesizers and two effects units, but the effects units are controlled by a MIDI foot pedal (or some other form of controller such as a computer) that enables the effects to be quickly and easily changed, independently of any program changes on the instruments. In this arrangement there are actually two MIDI pedal units, with the second one being used to provide program changes on the instruments. Although I said earlier that it was not possible to have two

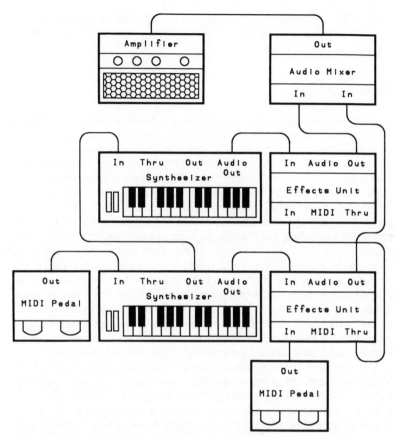

Figure 6.4 This MIDI system is actually two separate systems

MIDI controllers in a system without the aid of a merge unit, this is
one possible exception. The first instrument, on receiving a program
change message from the pedal unit might transmit this on to the second instrument. This is not a foregone conclusion though, and looking at the MIDI specifications of my instruments, none of them seem
to be able to operate in this way. This would result in the setup of Fig.
6.4 only providing program changes on the first instrument. To get
the program change messages through to the second instrument as
well it would then be necessary to feed the IN socket of this instrument from both the OUT and THRU sockets of the first instrument,
using a merge unit to combine the two signals. For live performances

123

with MIDI systems a MIDI pedal unit or some other quick source of program change messages could prove to be a 'how did I ever manage without it' piece of gear!

Basic sequencing

This is another application where using a MIDI connection between each piece of equipment might not be the best way of handling things. Suppose that an instrument having a built-in sequencer is used to provide a backing. This could be either a short repetitive track, or a long and complex type. In either case it could be programmed into the instrument, and then played back as required. Playing along with the backing does not require any MIDI link between the instrument you are playing and the one used to provide the accompaniment. If the instrument providing the backing is a drum machine, this still applies equally well. After all, the original intention was for instruments of this type to be stand-alone units used in this manner. A useful point to bear in mind is that most suitably equipped instruments can be played simultaneously from their keyboard and the built-in sequencer. Consequently, it may not be necessary to have two instruments in order to have a recorded backing and 'live' playing. However, this may only be realistic with a 16 note polyphonic instrument, as one having eight (or less) note polyphony might run out of voices.

It can be useful to program drum machines from a velocity sensitive MIDI keyboard rather than from the drum machine's own operating buttons (which are often not touch sensitive). Of course, MIDI drum pads are an alternative that most drummers would prefer. The drum machine should be supplied with a chart showing which drums correspond to which notes, so that you know which keys to play. It would be nice to have the ability to set each drum to respond to any desired note, but you are unlikely to have this feature available. With drum pads it should be possible to assign each one to any desired MIDI channel and note number, so that each one can be set to control any of the available drums. A drawback with some drum machines is that they can not be programmed via their MIDI inputs, only played by way of an external MIDI controller.

Sync link
A MIDI link becomes essential when two or more sequencers are to be used together. The type of setup we are talking about here is where two instruments with built-in sequencers are to be used together, and they must be kept in synchronization. These would typically be a

synthesizer having a built-in sequencer plus a drum machine. One sequencer must act as the controller and provide the timing clock messages, and the other sequencer or sequencers in the system must synchronize to this signal. This gives a standard MIDI controller and slave(s) arrangement which can utilize the star or chain method of connection. The timing messages are system types, and the slave sequencers should respond to them regardless of what mode or channel they are set to. Remember that apart from MIDI timing messages the controlling sequencer will also be transmitting its note sequence. Presumably in most cases the other instruments in the system will be sequenced through their own songs, and must ignore any note or other channel messages from the master sequencer. They way to achieve this is to have the slaves in the system set for mode 3 or mode 4 operation, and set to channels on which the master unit is not transmitting. You can have an instrument in the system follow the note messages from the controller to give thicker sounds if desired, but this instrument is then set to act as a standard slave type. Any internal sequencer it has is not used.

Step-time sequencing

Much step-time (and real-time) sequencing is done with everything in the system controlled from the master (and only) sequencer. There is a danger that with everything controlled from a single unit the MIDI data stream could become overloaded, but in practice quite complex scores can be sequenced without difficulties. However, it may be necessary to avoid polyphonic pitch bend or other facilities that generate massive amounts of data. There are countless permutations possible with modern MIDI instruments fed from a powerful step-time sequencer. The sequencer may well provide polyphonic operation on all 16 MIDI channels, but it could be difficult to furnish it with instruments to fully exploit this potential. Even with plenty of memory, complex 16 note polyphonic sequences might need to be very short!

The simplest solution is to have a 16 channel multi-timbral instrument that supports mode 4 operation. I suppose that instruments that can occupy all sixteen MIDI channels are still something of a rarity. Two 8 channel multi-timbral instruments in mode 4 or a multi mode are perhaps a more practical proposition, and would give an extremely versatile setup. The only point to bear in mind is that mode 4 is strictly a mono mode, and that there is no point in sequencing more than one note per channel. Either some notes will be ignored, or some will be terminated prematurely in order to make way for others. This is where a multi mode offers superior performance, and is well worth having.

The capabilities of multi modes vary from one instrument to another, and you must check the MIDI implementation charts for your instrument to determine how many notes per channel can be provided. Even with a fairly basic multi mode the scope of the system can be greatly increased. A basic multi mode offers something like eight note polyphony which can be used in the form of two notes per channel on four channels, four notes per channel on two channels, or straightforward mode 3/4 operation. A more sophisticated multi mode would have something like 16 to 32 note polyphony, plus dynamic voice allocation with up to eight notes per channel on up to eight channels. In other words, the instrument would operate as eight mode 3 virtual instruments on separate MIDI channels, with each one being eight note polyphonic, but with an overall limit of 16 to 32 notes at any one time. Even a single instrument of this type offers tremendous music making potential, and a good multi mode really is a great asset for sequencing work.

You can sometimes utilize mode 4 a little better by setting a few voices to the same program, and then effectively using these as a polyphonic instrument. This might not be very practical as it does not make very good use of the available channels, and it is inconvenient in that each note in a chord must be placed on a different track and channel. A more practical solution might be to have one instrument in mode 4 to provide something like eight monophonic tracks, and another instrument in mode 3 to provide sixteen note polyphonic track. This dodge is still a useful one for situations where the sixteen note limitation is not going to be restrictive.

Sound samplers sometimes have the ability to use different voices, depending on the velocity value in received note on messages. The idea behind this is to sample a sound at various levels of loudness, and to use the most appropriate sample for the velocity value present in each 'note on' that is received (a system used to good effect in some sampled electronic pianos). This is probably not well suited to anything other than its intended application.

A similar system which can often be used with sound samplers is to change voices depending on the note value. This is something that is designed to give more accurate results over a wide compass, and is another feature that is used to good effect with some electronic pianos. This can be useful when sequencing, since it gives two polyphonic tracks on a single MIDI channel. The two voices used do not normally have to be similar sounds, and you could have something like bowed double basses on the lower section of the split, and a penny-whistle on the upper section if that is really what you want! It might even be possible to have more than two zones, and then it would be possible for the sampler to take on the role of more than two instruments, albeit with each one having only a restricted compass.

MIDI complex

There are obviously a large number of ways in which the 16 available MIDI channels can be used when undertaking step-time sequencing. The more tracks and notes per track the sequencer can handle, the greater the possibilities. In practice it is unlikely to be the sequencer that is the limiting factor, and it will almost certainly be the number and quality of the instruments you can afford to connect to it that sets

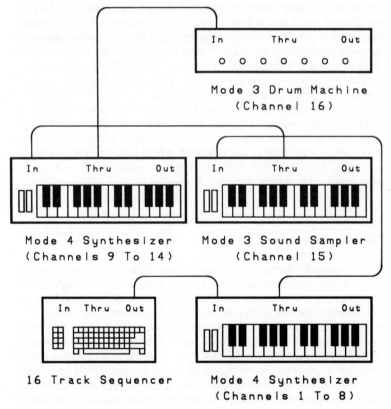

Figure 6.5 If you can afford it, some sophisticated MIDI sequencing setups are possible. This one is monophonic on 14 tracks, and polyphonic on the other two

the confines of the system. Fig. 6.5 shows the type of arrangement that could be set up with a suitably sophisticated system.

Having flexible instruments of the type described above, where there is plenty of choice as to exactly how the voices are assigned, really is a tremendous asset. Ideally, where an instrument has mode 3 it should be possible to assign it to any channel, or with a multiple mode 3 it should be possible to set it to any channels. Mode 4 is often a little restrictive in that it is usually only possible to use contiguous channels (which is what the MIDI specification seems to demand), and flexible mode 3 implementations might be needed to fit voices into gaps left by a mode 4 instrument. With compliant instruments and a little ingenuity it should be possible to reorganize the system to provide a voice arrangement to suit practically any requirements.

If you have a step time sequencer that enables controller and program change messages to be inserted at the required points, it should be possible to program some subtle changes into the voices of the instruments to help humanize the sound a little. Detailed sequencing of this type remains a dream for most of us though. This seems to be a very simple feature compared with the overall sophistication of most sequencer programs, but few seem to provide any facility of this type.

It is not essential to use complex multi-channel setups when undertaking step-time sequencing, and if your main interest is (say) piano music, then a sequencer and a MIDI equipped electronic piano in mode 1 should be all that are required. MIDI has the potential to do much more than this, but it can be applied equally well to a simple arrangement of this type if that is all you require.

Real-time sequencing

During playback, there is really very little difference (if any) between step-time and real-time sequencing. Equipment and configurations that will give good results in one application should work well in the other. Remember that with a MIDI multi-track recording system you can not use the same instrument over and over again, as is often done when building up a complex piece using multi-track tape recording. In order to reproduce the final piece you must have an instrument or one voice of an instrument matched to each track. MIDI recording brings benefits in terms of greatly enhanced editing capabilities and avoiding the need for extremely expensive tape recording equipment, but for really good results with complex sequences a selection of high quality instruments are needed.

The real difference between step-time and real-time sequencing is the method of entering sequences into the computer (or dedicated sequencer). With step-time sequencing you need no more than the facilities of the sequencer to program a song, although there may be the option of entering data from a keyboard instrument. With real-time sequencing the music is entered only from the keyboard (or a MIDI guitar, or other controlling device). Assuming that conventional keyboard control will be used, either a good quality MIDI keyboard is needed, or an instrument having a touch-sensitive keyboard of respectable quality is required. The real-time sequencing equivalent of Fig. 6.4 would be virtually the same. The only difference would be the addition of a MIDI cable from the OUT socket of the keyboard to the IN socket of the sequencer.

In command

If you set up a complex MIDI system it would be naive to expect to fully master it within a couple of hours. It will probably take longer than that to read through the manuals and reach the stage where you are ready to connect up and switch on. Modern electronic instruments and sequencers are highly capable and versatile pieces of equipment, but that versatility inevitably means that there is a lot to learn. Try simple setups first, and be prepared to experiment. There should be no risk of damaging anything unless you somehow get two MIDI OUT sockets (or THRU types) wired together. Even if this should happen, the current limiting resistors at the outputs should prevent any damage from occurring.

Probably most users who have complex MIDI systems started out with a much more basic system, and gradually expanded it as they gained more experience and saw new possibilities. This is not necessarily the best way of handling things in that you can soon outgrow equipment, and trading it in for something more appropriate can be an expensive business. On the other hand, it is better than spending a large sum of money on an up-market system and giving up when you can not learn to drive it.

Try, try, again
You may not always get the desired result at the first attempt, but be prepared to read through the manuals again as you may well discover an alternative approach that will bear fruit. You may not always be able to get the system to provide exactly the functions you require, and

compromises may have to be accepted. Even a compromised MIDI system should still be pretty powerful, and well worth using.

The real stumbling block for many users of computer based systems is learning to use the software, rather than any problems in getting everything set up and ready to go. When I first started using word processors and computer aided drawing programs I found it difficult to get information into the computer properly, and all but impossible to get anything usable on to paper. This was not due to any fault in the software, but was simply due to the fact that after a lifetime of doing things one way it is difficult to suddenly adopt a whole new approach. During the transition it will probably take a long time to produce very little. After a few weeks you will probably wonder how you managed to tackle the job without a computer, and with good software you will use the system largely intuitively.

When trying to design a system to suit your requirements, probably the best approach is to go mentally through the basic steps of using the system, making a note of what equipment is needed, and what features that equipment must have. Then try to find the equipment that best matches up with these requirements.

Manuals

It is more or less standard practice for MIDI equipment to be supplied with two manuals, or possibly a single manual in two distinct sections. One is the usual information on how to connect it up, set the required modes, and other general information on using the unit. The second one gives technical information including full details of the MIDI implementation. This is normally in two sections, with one detailing transmitted messages, and the other listing received messages that are recognized. This is essential reading for the MIDI user, as it is only with this information that you can decide how best to set up and exploit the equipment.

Much of this information is pretty straightforward, and should give no real difficulties. It will probably list 'note on', 'note off' messages, etc., with the binary code numbers for each one. Read the fine print as this will usually contain some important information. For example, the mono mode change message may well be recognized, but its effect may be no more than to switch off all notes (i.e. modes 2 and 4 will not be available). This should also detail any messages that are only transmitted or received if they are enabled via the appropriate command from the front panel controls. There should also be information on how to enable and disable the sending and acceptance of these MIDI messages, which are likely to include program change messages and possibly MIDI timing messages. This is often possible using system exclusive messages, but in practice the front panel controls might be the only means of control.

Other information to look for is whether variable controllers use the full 14 bit resolution. There should also be details of what function (if any) is assigned to each MIDI controller. This might be a nice and easy to understand list, but in some of the manuals I have seen this information has been provided in the form of tables that are more like something out of a puzzle book than part of an instruction manual!

If you are using instruments for sequencing it is important to look up their usable note range. Few instruments (if any) cover the full 0 to 127 range, but most cover quite a wide compass when receiving notes. The transmitted note range is often different, and more restricted. If equipment supports mode 3 and (or) mode 4, the specification sheet should indicate which channels can be used, and how to set the equipment to the desired channels if channel assignment is user-adjustable.

There are often some useful extras available using system exclusive messages. However, these will probably only be usable if you have other items of equipment from the same manufacturer. Although MIDI has gone a long way to providing a true standard that lets you 'mix and match' equipment from various manufacturers without any difficulties, there can still be advantages in building up a system using equipment from a single manufacturer.

One point worth emphasizing again is that the MIDI specification will only detail messages that the equipment can send and interpret when received. It will not list the MIDI messages that are not implemented, and it is up to you to look for any serious omissions.

The future

MIDI is now so well established that it is unlikely that it will be superseded in the near future, or for many years to come. It is sufficiently flexible to accommodate new developments, and is currently working well with a wide range of equipment. The only really serious criticism aimed at MIDI is its inability to handle large amounts of data in a short space of time, leading to occasional signal bottlenecks on some complicated setups. One solution which might eventually evolve is a 'turbo' MIDI mode operating at a higher baud rate, so that faster data transfer could be achieved with suitable equipment. This could be a worthwhile development, but the control electronics in MIDI equipment might need to be improved considerably in order to be able to fully utilize such a mode. The problem at present is not just that the MIDI data stream becomes overloaded, but also that equipment can receive data faster than it can handle it, leading to malfunctions.

A likely development is an increase in the number of MIDI controllable devices available, and units designed to process a MIDI signal to give special effects. This is an area that is so far largely unexplored. The MIDI world should certainly be an interesting one for many years to come.

There are a number of proposals at present under consideration that would extend the capabilities of MIDI. These would seem to be additions to the standard, rather than changes to existing methods. This would presumably ensure that any new instruments having these extra facilities would maintain a high level of compatibility with older instruments. The new proposals include the ability to send bar numbers within a MIDI clock stream, the ability to request a system exclusive patch dump from an unknown synthesiser, and the ability to send standard MIDI files via MIDI. As far as I am aware, at the time of writing this none of these proposals has been officially adopted as part of the MIDI standard.

Appendix 1
MIDI modes

Mode no.	New name	Old name	Characteristics
1	Omni on/poly	Omni	Responds to notes on all channels polyphonically
2	Omni on/mono	None	Responds to notes on all channels monophonically
3	Omni off/poly	Poly	Responds to notes on one channel polyphonically
4	Omni off/mono	Mono	Responds to notes on one channel monophonically
Multi	None	None	Multiple mode 3 operation

Other modes are manufacturers' own, and non-standard.

Appendix 2
Hexadecimal numbers

In addition to binary numbers you will often find hexadecimal numbers in MIDI equipment manuals. In most cases you will not need to understand these, but it is possible that the numbers for controllers and programs will be given only in this numbering system. You may then need to convert them to decimal numbers in order to tie them in with other pieces of equipment. The hexadecimal numbering system is not too difficult to understand, and the general idea is to have a single digit to replace four binary bits. An 8 bit byte can therefore be represented by a two digit hexadecimal (or 'hex') number. This system works well with MIDI messages where many of the bytes are divided into two 4 bit nibbles, as each nibble can be represented by a single hexadecimal digit.

Each nibble covers a range of 0 to 16 in decimal numbering, and there are obviously too few single digit numbers in this system to accommodate the hexadecimal system. The solution to this problem is to augment the ten normal numbers with the first six letters of the alphabet (A to F). It is from this that the hexadecimal name is derived. The table shows the relationship between each of the hexadecimal digits and both decimal and binary numbers.

Converting binary numbers to hexadecimal is not difficult, and it is just a matter of looking up the corresponding hexadecimal digit for each nibble. For instance, the binary number 11110101 breaks down into the nibbles 1111 and 0101. These correspond to the hexadecimal digits F and 5, giving an answer of F5. Conversion in the opposite direction is just as simple, and it is just a matter of looking up the binary values for each of the hexadecimal digits, and then combining these to produce a single binary number. For example, A7 in hex corresponds to the binary numbers 1010 (A) and 0111 (7), giving an answer of 10100111. The conversion you are most likely to need is from hexadecimal to decimal. This is again reasonably straightforward, and

Hexadecimal	Binary	Decimal
0	0000	0
1	0001	1
2	0010	2
3	0011	3
4	0100	4
5	0101	5
6	0110	6
7	0111	7
8	1000	8
9	1001	9
A	1010	10
B	1011	11
C	1100	12
D	1101	13
E	1110	14
F	1111	15

it is a matter of first looking up the corresponding decimal number for the most significant digit and then multiplying this by 16. Then look up the corresponding decimal number for the least significant digit, and add this to the value obtained for the most significant digit. As an example, to convert 4E in hexadecimal to decimal, first the most significant digit (4) is converted to decimal (still 4) and is then multiplied by 16, which gives an answer of 64. Then the least significant digit (E) is converted to decimal (14) and added to the previous answer. This gives 64 plus 14, which gives a final answer of 78.

Appendix 3
Useful addresses

Magazines (UK)

Keyboard Review, Alexander House, Forehill, Ely, Cambs CB7 4AF

Keyboard Player, 330 Hertford Road, London N9 7HB

Making Music, 20 Bowling Green Lane, London EC1R 0BD

MIDI Monitor, UKMA, 26 Brunswick Park Gardens, London N11 1EJ

Music Technology, Alexander House, Forehill, Ely, Cambs CB7 4AF

Sound on Sound, PO Box 30, St Ives, Cambs PE17 4XQ

Manufacturers (UK)

Akai UK, Haslemere Heathrow Estate, Silver Jubilee Way, Parkway, Hounslow, Middx TW4 6NQ (Tel 081–897 6388)

Alesis, see Sound Technology

Atari, Atari House, Railway Terrace, Slough, Berks SL25BZ, (Tel 0753 33344)

Bluebridge Music, 3/5 Fourth Avenue, Bluebridge Ind Estate, Halstead, Essex CO9 2SY (Tel 0787 475325)

Boss, see Roland

Casio Electronics Co Limited, Unit 6, 1000 North Circular Road, London NW2 7JD (Tel 081–450 9131)

Cheetah International, Norbury House, Norbury Road, Fairwater, Cardiff CF5 38S (Tel 0222 555525)

Commodore, Commodore House, The Switchback, Gardner Road, Maidenhead, Berks SL6 7XA (Tel 0628 770088)

Electromusic Research, 14 Mount Close, Wickford, Essex SS11 8HG (Tel 0702 335747)

Emu Systems, PO Box 1, Prestonpans, East Lothian, EH32 0TT (Tel 0875 813330)

Ensoniq UK, Ensoniq House, Mirage Estate, Hodgson Way, Wickford Essex SS11 8YL (Tel 0268 561177)

Farfisa UK, Fraser Street, Burnley, Lancs BB1 1UL (Tel 0282 35431)

John Hornby Skewes, Salem House, Garforth, Leeds LS25 1PX (Tel 0532 865381)

Kawai UK, Sun Alliance House, 8–10 Dean Park Cresent, Bournemouth BH1 1HL (Tel 0202 296629)

Korg UK, 8–9 The Crystal Centre, Elm Grove Road, Harrow, MIddx HA1 2YR (Tel 0181–427 5377)

Oberheim, see Sound Technology

Philip Rees, Unit B, Park End Works, Croughton, Brackley, Northants NN13 5LX (Tel 0869 810948)

Roland (UK) Limited, Amalgamated Drive, West Cross Centre, Brentford, Middx TW8 9EZ (Tel 081–568 1247)

Rosetti, 4 Tamdown Way, Springwood Ind Estate, Braintree, Essex CM7 7QL (Tel 0376 550033)

Sound Technology, Unit 15, Letchworth Point, Dunhams Lane, Letchworth, Herts SG6 1ND (Tel 0462 480000)

Yamaha, Mount Avenue, Bletchley, Milton Keynes MK1 1JE (Tel 0908 371771)

Other organizations (UK)

Akai Active, Haslemere Heathrow Estate, Silver Jubilee Way, Parkway, Hounslow, Middx TW4 6NQ (Tel 081–897 6388)

Mirage User Group, 2 Walnut Tree Cottages, The Green, Frant, E Sussex TN3 9DE

Roland Newslink, Roland (UK), West Cross Centre, Brentford, Middx TW8 9EZ (Tel 081–568 1247)

Roland User Groups, Stage One, 26 Soper Grove, Basingstoke, Hants RG21 2PU

Steinberg User Club, 68 Wilsdon Way, Kidlington, Oxford OX5 1TX

The Music Network, see Sound on Sound magazine

UK MIDI Association, 26 Brunswick Park Gardens, London N11 1EJ (Tel 081 368 3667 Fax 081 368 7918)

Magazines (USA and Canada)

Canadian Musician, 832 Mount Pleasant Road, Toronto, Ontario M4P 2L3

Electronic Musician Magazine, 2608 Ninth Street, Berkeley, CA 94710

International Musician, Suite 600, Paramount Building, 1501 Broadway, NY 10036

Keyboard, 20085 Stevens Creek, Cupertino, CA 95014

Mix Magazine, 2608 Ninth Street, Berkeley, CA 94710

Modern Drummer, 870 Pompton Avenue, Cedar Grove, New Jersey 07009

Music, Computers and Software, 190 East Main Street, Huntingdon, NY

Music & Sound Output, 25 Willowdale Ave, Port Washington, NY 11050

Music Technology, 7361 Topanga Canyon Blvd., Canoga Park, CA 91303

Musician, 1515 Broadway, 39th Floor, NY 10036

Percussion, 6 Avenue J, Brooklyn, NY 11230

Manufacturers (USA)

Akai Professional, PO Box 2344, Fort Worth, Texas, TX 76113

Alesis, PO Box 3908, Los Angeles, CA 90078

Casio, 15 Gardner Road, Fairfield, NJ 07006

EMU Systems, 1600 Green Hills Road, Scotts Valley, CA 95066

Ensoniq, 155 Great Valley Parkway, Malvern, PA 19355

Fairlight, 2945 Westwood Blvd., Los Angeles, CA 90064

Fostex, 15431 Blackburn Ave, Norwalk, CA 90650

Kawai America, 2055 East University Drive, PO Box 9045, Compton, CA 90224

Korg USA, 89 Frost Street, Westbury, NY 11590

Kurzweil Music Systems, 411 Waverley Oaks Road, Waltham, MA 02154

Oberheim, 11650 W. Olympic Blvd, Los Angeles, CA 90064

RolandCorp US, 7200 Dominion Circle, Los Angeles, CA 90040

Simmons USA, 23917 Craftsman Road, Calabasas, CA 91302

Yamaha, PO Box 6600, Buena Park, CA 90622

Other organizations (USA)

International MIDI Association, 5316 West 57th Street, Los Angeles, CA 90056, USA, Tel 010 213 649 6434, Fax 0101 213 215 3380

MIDI Manufacturer's Association, 5316 West 57th Street Los Angeles, CA 90056, USA, Tel 0101 213 649 6434, Fax 0101 213 215 3380

Roland User Group, c/o Roland Corp US, 7200 Dominion Circle Los Angeles, CA 90040

Appendix 4
Glossary

Active sensing
Not many MIDI devices seem to implement this feature. The basic idea is for a MIDI active sensing message to be periodically sent by the MIDI controller. If a broken cable or something of this nature results in a breakdown in communications, the controlled equipment will detect the absence of the active sensing messages, and will switch off all notes. Otherwise, any notes that are left switched on will remain so indefinitely.

Baud
This is the speed at which data is transmitted in a serial data system (such as MIDI). MIDI operates at 31250 baud (or 31.25 kilobaud), which means that with a continuous stream of data some 31250 bits of information per second are sent. This is not quite as good as it might at first appear, since ten bits (including timing bits) per byte are required, and typically three bytes per MIDI message are needed. This works out at around one thousand MIDI messages per second. This is adequate for most purposes, but with complex systems it is possible for MIDI to become overloaded.

Binary
A form of numbering system where the only digits used are 0 and 1. This may seem a bit crude, but it is the system used in all digital electronics, and MIDI sends values in the form of binary numbers.

Bit
Bit is an abbreviation for 'binary digit', which is the basic unit of information used in a digital system (such as MIDI).

Byte
Digital systems normally operate on 8 bits of data at a time, and a group of eight bits is a byte. Even with a system such as MIDI where data is sent one bit at a time, the bits are still grouped into 8 bit bytes.

Chain connection
See 'THRU'.

Channel
MIDI can operate on up to 16 channels that are normally simply called channels 1 to 16. Many MIDI messages carry a channel number, and can be selected by just one instrument (mode 3) or one voice of an instrument (mode 4). Note that any equipment set with 'omni on' will simply ignore channel numbers and respond to all messages.

Channel messages
These are simply the MIDI messages that carry a channel number in the header byte, and which can therefore be directed to one instrument, or one voice of an instrument. These messages include such things as note on, note off, and program change instructions. Messages that do not contain a channel number are called system messages.

Clock
A clock signal (in electronic music) is a regular series of electronic pulses sent from one sequencer to another in order to keep the two units properly synchronized (a system which is mainly associated with drum machines). In MIDI, the clock signal is a regular series of MIDI clock messages, rather than just a simple series of pulses.

Controller (1)
MIDI controller messages enable individual controls of an instrument or other piece of MIDI equipment to be adjusted. For example, they can be used to vary the parameters of an ADSR envelope shaper (variable controllers), or to permit the low frequency modulation to be switched on and off (switch controllers).

Controller (2)
A MIDI controller is also any device that transmits MIDI codes, and which can therefore control other MIDI equipment. Originally MIDI controllers were keyboards, but these days there are computer based controllers, foot pedals, guitar controllers, and various other types. You do not have to be a keyboard player in order to exploit the power of MIDI.

Copy protection
This is where a software producer uses some system of data encoding (or whatever) to prevent program disks and tapes from being copied. The idea is to prevent people from copying software bought by their friends rather than buying their own (legitimate) copy. Some disks are copyable, but the copies will not load and run properly. Another method, and one that is popular with the more expensive programs, is to have a 'dongle', or 'security key'. This is an electronic device which connects to one of the computer's ports. Dongled software can be copied, but will not run without the right dongle connected to the computer. The use of copy protection and similar methods by the software publishers is quite understandable. On the other hand, it can be inconvenient to users who are presumably paying any extra costs involved.

Delay
Some sequencers have a delay facility, which enables data for one track to be sent slightly delayed relative to data for another track. The idea of this is to permit instruments to be properly synchronized when one responds more rapidly to data than another. This is not an effect I have encountered, but a delay facility is presumably more than a little useful with a system that does suffer from this problem. Significant delays are sometimes introduced (so it is said) when data passes from an 'IN' socket to a 'THRU' socket. With a large system using the chain method of connection it is corrupted data rather than significant delays that would seem to be the main danger.

DIN connector
This is the standard type of plug/socket used for MIDI interconnections. Note that it is no good trying to buy just any DIN connector, as there are numerous types. The variety used for MIDI interconnections is the 5 way 180 degree type.

Disk
A computer disk is a device for magnetically storing data (sound samples, songs for a sequencer, etc.), and a disk drive is the hardware that records data on to and reads it back from a disk. Disks enable libraries of data to be built up, and provide a reasonably permanent form of storage (remember that the memories of many instruments and virtually all computers are completely lost when the power is switched off). Cassette recorders are often used as a cheap alternative to disk drives, but are slower and less convenient.

Event

A MIDI event is merely a MIDI message of some kind. Sequencers often have their storage capacity specified as a certain number of events. As note on and note off commands are separate events, and after-touch or other messages may be involved, the maximum note capacity is likely to be less than half the maximum number of events that can be accommodated.

Expander

A MIDI expander is an instrument that has no keyboard and can only be played via its MIDI IN socket and an external keyboard or other controller. Sounds are sometimes preset and non-adjustable, but some of the more recent units are quite versatile. Originally intended as add-ons for organs, the better expanders potentially have much wider application.

Filter

A MIDI filter is not an audio filter that is controlled by way of MIDI signals. It is a device that connects into the MIDI cable and blocks certain types of message from its output. For example, a filter could be added ahead of an instrument that has only omni modes and will respond to messages on all channels. By removing all channel messages except those on a particular channel, the instrument could effectively be used in mode 3.

Hard disk (fixed disk)

Normal computer disks are often called floppy disks, as the disk on which magnetic coating is deposited is far from rigid. A hard disk is a more sophisticated type where the disk is rigid, rotates continuously at high speed, and cannot be removed from the drive. The non-interchangeability of the disks is not a major drawback, as the capacity of a hard disk is typically equal to that of about 60 floppy disks. The point of a hard disk is that it gives very rapid access to vast amounts of data. An increasingly popular feature on up-market computers, and also to be found on some of the more recent sound samplers.

Hardware

Hardware is simply any piece of electronic equipment, including computers and musical instruments. Data or programs used by the equipment is the 'software'. Data or programs held on ROM are sometimes referred to as 'firmware', presumably because they are a combination of software (the data in the ROM) and hardware (the ROM itself)!

Hexadecimal (hex)
Hexadecimal is a system of numbering based on 16 (rather than ten like the ordinary decimal sytstem). The normal numeric digits from 0 to 9 are augmented by the first six letters of the alphabet (A to F) in order to give the 16 different single digit numbers required by the system. Equipment manuals often give MIDI codes in hexadecimal form, but usually include a conversion table that gives hex to decimal conversions.

Icon
See 'WIMP'.

Kilobyte (k)
The storage capacity of computer disks and memory circuits is often quoted in kilobytes, or just as so many 'k'. A kilobyte is 1000 bytes of data, or, if you wish to be pedantic, 1024 bytes.

Librarian
This is a computer program that stores sets of voice data for synthesizers or other instruments. It enables the required sounds to be quickly selected and loaded from disk and transmitted to the instrument via MIDI.

Megabyte
The capacity of large memory circuits and high capacity disks is often quoted in megabytes. A megabyte is equivalent to 1024 k, or 1048576 bytes.

MIDI choke
A term used to describe what happens if a system is called upon to transmit more data than MIDI can handle. Exactly what happens when MIDI choke occurs depends on the system, but at the very least it is likely that the timing of note on/off messages will be severely disrupted. In an extreme case it is possible that the MIDI controller would crash, and the system would be brought to a halt.

Mono
In a MIDI context 'mono' means that only one note per channel is possible. In MIDI mode 2 an instrument is truly monophonic as operation on only one voice is possible, but in mode 4 (formerly known as mono mode) it is possible for an instrument to operate monophonically on several channels. The instrument is then polyphonic, while it

is the MIDI channels that are monophonic. The term mono is perhaps a bit misleading in this respect.

Mouse
See 'WIMP'.

Notation program
Also called 'score writer' programs, these permit music to be written into the computer in standard music notation form. Some programs of this type are simply intended as a means of producing sheet music, but many now support MIDI, and will operate as step-time sequencers. In fact some will turn MIDI data into notes on the staves, and will operate as real-time sequencers (but will not necessarily work particularly well in this role).

Omni
When 'omni' is 'on', an instrument will respond to messages on any MIDI channel. When 'omni' is 'off', the instrument will only respond to one particular channel (mode 3), or each voice will be assigned to a particular channel (mode 4).

Pointer
In the sense of a song pointer, it is a MIDI message that moves a sequencer to a certain point in the sequence. As a computing term it means an on screen pointer (see 'WIMP').

Poly
In a polyphonic mode an instrument can handle several notes at once. In mode 3 it is possible to have polyphonic operation on each MIDI channel. The maximum number of notes available at one time is determined by the instruments—the MIDI specification does not set any upper limit.

Port
A port is merely some form of electrical connector on a computer or other piece of electronics to enable it to be connected to some peripheral device. MIDI IN, OUT, and THRU sockets are all examples of ports. The alternative term interface is sometimes used.

Printout
Some programs enable data to be printed via a suitable printer. This is very useful, expecially with something like a sequencer program that permits only a small portion of long sequences to be displayed on the

screen. Also useful with notation (score writer) programs where it enables conventional sheet music to be produced. However, for graphics output a graphics compatible printer is needed (most programs will work properly with any Epson compatible dot-matrix printer).

Program change
Most instruments and other items of MIDI equipment make use of 'programs'. In an instrument, for example, these are a series of preset control settings that give a range of different sounds. Program change messages therefore permit the required sounds to be selected at the appropriate times. Other items of MIDI equipment such as mixers and effects units are often controlled via program change messages.

Program dump
Many MIDI equipped instruments have the ability to send out via MIDI the full contents of their program memory, or to provide a 'program dump'. This can be used to send a set of programs from one instrument to another (but they will normally need to be instruments of exactly the same type). This facility can also be used to send data to a computer or MIDI disk drive, and then feed it back again when and as required. There is no special MIDI program dump message, and this facility operates under system exclusive messages.

Qwerty keyboard
A term which seems to confuse a lot of people, it simply refers to a typewriter style keyboard (as used in expanded form on virtually all computers). 'Qwerty' is the first six letters on the top row of letters keys.

RAM
This is an acronym for random access memory. If you program an instrument (or a computer) this is the electronic circuit that is used to store the information. The contents of RAM are lost when the power is switched off, but many instruments have a battery to power the RAM after switch-off so that contents of the memory are retained. I have not encountered any computers with the ability to store more than very limited amounts of memory in this 'battery-backed' RAM.

Real-time sequencer
A sequencer where the music is entered into the unit simply by playing it on a MIDI keyboard. The sequencer records the data from the keyboard, which is stored in its memory together with timing information. The ability to change the playback speed is a standard feature.

The more up-market systems permit note values and durations to be edited, and multi-track sequences to be built up.

ROM
ROM stands for read only memory. As this name suggests, once the contents of ROM have been set at the manufacturing stage they cannot be altered. The main point about ROM is that it retains its contents when the power is switched off (unlike ordinary RAM). ROM is used for storing data and (or) programs that will be needed frequently. RAM (see above) is what is needed for storing your own data and programs.

Serial
MIDI is a form of serial communications system, which simply means that it sends information one 'bit' at a time. Parallel systems send data several 'bits' at a time, and are usually much faster. They need multi-way connecting cables though, and often have very restricted ranges (a couple of metres in some cases). Although slower, a serial system is more practical for many applications.

Software
Software originally meant computer programs in any form (on disk, tape, written down, or whatever). It seems to be more generalized nowadays, and sound samples for use in a sound sampler would be considered 'software'.

Star connection
See 'THRU-box'.

Step-time sequencer
This is a sequencer where the music is programmed by specifying the note value and duration in some way other than playing the music on to a MIDI keyboard and recording the MIDI output data plus timing information. A notation program where the music is placed on to an on-screen stave (or staves) in conventional music notation form is an up-market example of a step-time sequencer. With more simple types the notes are entered in a more simple form, such as 'C-2, 1/4 note' for instance. Great if your imagination out-performs your playing skills, but a relatively slow way of doing things.

System exclusive
The system exclusive messages are ones that are designed for use only by equipment from one manufacturer. The header byte includes an

identification number so that system exclusive messages from equipment of the wrong manufacturer can be filtered out and ignored. Virtually any feature can be implemented using system exclusive messages, and unlimited data can be included in each one of these!

System messages
These are the MIDI messages that do not carry a channel number in the header byte. They are therefore responded to by every piece of equipment in the system that recognizes them. These are mainly the MIDI clock and associated messages.

THRU
A THRU socket is to be found on many items of MIDI equipment. It simply provides a replica of what is received on the IN socket. In a multi-unit system the THRU socket on one unit can be coupled through to the IN socket of the next unit (chain connection).

THRU-box
Not all MIDI units have THRU sockets, and in particular, they are often absent from keyboard instruments. A THRU-box has a MIDI IN socket and several THRU output sockets. In a multi-unit system the OUT socket of the controller connects to the IN socket of the THRU-box. The THRU outputs then connect to the IN sockets of each instrument etc. in the system (star connection).

Voice editor
The minimalist approach to synthesizer controls has made setting up the required sounds a relatively long and difficult process. A voice editor program provides on-screen controls that can quickly and easily be adjusted. New control settings are almost instantly sent to the instrument via MIDI so that the effect of adjusting controls can be heard, and fine adjustments easily made.

Visual editor
A program for use with sound samplers, it draws out waveforms on the screen so that suitable start, end and loop points can be selected quickly and accurately. Relies on swapping sound sample information via MIDI system exclusive messages.

WIMP
WIMP is an acronym for Windows, Icons, Mouse, and Pointer. It is a means of controlling computer programs, where an on screen pointer is moved around the screen using a hand operated controller (the

mouse). The mouse and pointer are used to select options via icons, which are on-screen graphical representations (pictures of various instruments so you can select the one you wish to use for example). The windows are areas of the screen which are given over to different functions, or with some computers can even be used for different programs! A WIMP environment makes it easy for inexperienced users to operate complex programs, but only if the software is well designed and the computer is powerful enough to run it properly.

Window
See 'WIMP'.

Word
In a computer sense, this is a group of bits that is longer than a normal 8 bit byte. For example, with a 16 bit sound sampler, a memory capacity of 500 k words means that 500 k of full 16 bit words can be accommodated (which is equivalent to 1000 k bytes of storage).

XLR
This is a type of electrical connector used for MIDI interconnections on some equipment (generally units that are designed for rough handling on the road). Any supplier of MIDI equipment which uses this type of connector should be able to supply suitable connecting leads as well, together with adaptors to permit standard 5 way DIN MIDI leads to be used.

Index

Advanced MIDI User's Guide

RA Penfold

216 × 138 mm ★ illustrated ★
ISBN 1 870775 18 X ★ £9.95

- ★ Explains all the MIDI messages

- ★ Routing signals in simple to advanced systems

- ★ Covers the use of system exclusive messages

- ★ Explains how to troubleshoot when things go wrong

- ★ Shows how to use MIDI pedals and other gadgets

- ★ Explains MIDI time codes and synchronising with non MIDI kit

Although still regarded by many as nothing more than a means of getting one instrument to follow the playing of another, MIDI actually has capabilities that go well beyond this simple slaving arrangement. MIDI can be used as a means of storing and replaying complex pieces of music, for the control of sophisticated systems having more than a dozen instruments, and can even be used to control ancillary equipment such as mixers and effects units.

There seem to be few gadgets associated with electronic music which do not sport a set of MIDI sockets these days. MIDI has "come of age", and is crucial to

much of today's electronic music making. This book is for those who wish to go beyond very basic slaving and sequencer setups, and who wish to exploit MIDI to the full.

The topics covered include: MIDI modes and codes. MIDI signal routing and patch bays. System exclusive messages and their practical uses. MIDI trouble shooting, including the use of a computer as a diagnostic tool. MIDI gadgets – channelisers, filters, merge units, pedals, etc. Synchronisation – MIDI time code, SMPTE, etc. The basics of DIY MIDI programming. MIDI hardware specification.

Send your cheque for £10.45 (inc 50p P&P) payable to PC Publishing to:
PC Publishing, 4 Brook Street, Tonbridge, Kent TN9 2PJ Tel 0732 770893.

STEVE PROCTOR . HONNER .